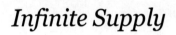

Infinite Supply

Books by Chip Brogden

Strength for the Journey
Why Do You Call Me Lord?
Infinite Supply
The Ekklesia
The Irresistible Kingdom
The Irresistible Life
Getting Babylon Out of You
Embrace the Cross

CHIP BROGDEN

infinite
supply

366 Daily Meditations for Christ-centered Living

Infinite Supply (*Second Edition*)
©2010 Chip Brogden

Published by The School of Christ
http://www.TheSchoolOfChrist.Org

Preface
to the Second Edition

Infinite Supply is more than a book of daily devotions – it is a doorway that opens up the heart and the mind to the immeasurable, unsearchable, unending treasure of spiritual blessing that is found in the Person of Jesus Christ.

We began mailing short daily messages to our email list in 2003, and these messages were compiled into print a few years after that. This second print edition of *Infinite Supply* features easy-to-read type; simplified Scripture references; new, updated content from my more recent writings; and a collection of inspirational and motivational quotes.

The source material for this book is primarily drawn from two other books in print: *The Irresistible Kingdom* and *Embrace the Cross*. The rest of the content is taken from the original email messages and longer articles and essays, many of which are still available in full at TheSchoolOfChrist.Org.

We believe that Jesus Christ is Infinite Supply. These writings represent our best effort at representing Him and His Kingdom. We wish you every spiritual blessing as you start each new day with a Christ-centered focus from *Infinite Supply*!

Chip Brogden
Canandaigua, New York
November, 2010

January 1

"According to the eternal purpose which
He accomplished in Christ Jesus our Lord."
EPHESIANS 3:11

When we really look at what the Bible says and grasp the implications of the Gospel according to Jesus then we soon discover that this Good News is better than we could have ever dared to hope. It is a story of recovering something that was once thought to be totally lost, redeeming something that was once thought to be absolutely hopeless. It is a story of God bringing something wonderfully good out of something terribly evil. It is a story of God bringing Life and Light out of so much death and darkness. It is a story of love, and the incredible lengths to which that Love will go to secure the object of its affection.

The Gospel is more, so much more, than how to avoid hell and go to heaven; it is the story of an Idea, a Purpose, an Intention, a Plan, which is working itself out in this universe even as you sit here reading these words.

January 2

"Come, take up the cross, and follow Me."
MARK 10:21

What does it really mean to be crucified with Christ? Thankfully, God does not ask us to submit to physical crucifixion in order to prove that we are disciples of Jesus. When Jesus tells us to take up our Cross and follow Him, He is not telling us that we must pay the penalty for our sins. Thank God that Jesus has paid the penalty for us! Taking up the Cross, for us, is adopting a spiritual attitude of self-denial, of surrender, and of yielding all that we have and all that we are to God.

Although that aspect of the Cross occurs in us day by day and moment by moment, what Christ accomplished through His death on the Cross is finished, complete, and settled once and for all. This finished work of the Cross is the basis upon which we can take up the Cross daily and follow after Him.

January 3

"I have heard of You by the hearing of
the ear, but now my eye sees You."
JOB 42:5

The testing of Job was a valid test, a crucial one, and a crucible through which each Christian will be purged, sifted, and tried. To what end? It is summed up in the words of Job himself as he neared the end of his ordeal: "I have heard of You by the hearing of the ear: but now my eye sees You." BUT NOW! BUT NOW! BUT NOW! Before he heard about Him, but now he sees Him, and falls to the ground. Before he worshipped Him having heard, now he worships having seen, and known.

I believe that God set him up for such experiential knowledge by allowing him to be subjected to the assaults of the devil, the harshness of his environment, the mis-understanding of his friends, the loss of his family and material possessions, and his physical infirmity. I submit that if anyone desires to take up the Cross and follow Christ, such testing is the only realistic expectation His disciple can entertain.

January 4

"Take up the whole armor of God,
that you may be able to withstand in the evil day,
and having done all, to stand."
EPHESIANS 6:13

I f we see the devil as defeated then we will not fight, we will stand. If we see ourselves as earthly then we will behave in an earthly manner: our words, our thoughts, our prayers, our deeds, our warfare will be carried out in an earthly manner. If we see ourselves seated with Christ in the heavenlies then we will behave in a heavenly manner, as a heavenly people, bringing the Mind and Will and Kingdom of God to bear upon that which is contrary to Christ on the earth.

How do we obtain heavenly vision? We must ask to see as He sees. We must pray that God will illuminate our heart. Our vision affects our actions.

January 5

"To you it has been given to know
the mysteries of the kingdom of God, but to
the rest it is given in parables."
LUKE 8:10

T he parables are not quaint little stories;
they are prophetic declarations of spiritual
truth, and they give us invaluable insight into
this Irresistible Kingdom.

Concealing the truth within the context of a
parable was necessary, Jesus said, because "To
you [the disciples] it has been given to know
the mysteries of the kingdom of heaven, but to
the rest it is given in parables."

Those who want to understand the mysteries
of the Kingdom have to have a relationship
with the King. The mysteries of the Kingdom
are reserved, not for passive listeners, but for
true followers: so "when they were alone, He
explained all things to His disciples" (Mark
4:34).

January 6

"Though He was crucified in weakness,
yet He lives by the power of God. For we also are
weak in Him, but we shall live with Him
by the power of God."
2 CORINTHIANS 13:4

As we daily embrace the Cross we will discover that the truth of our freedom in Christ becomes more real to us than the sin that used to imprison us. We will learn that the Cross is not a mere theory, philosophy, or theological teaching; the Cross is a very real, practical, spiritual principle of Life overcoming Death, Light overcoming Darkness, and God's Power being revealed in the midst of our weakness.

January 7

"This is your hour, and the
power of darkness."
LUKE 22:53

Despised and rejected of men, betrayed by Judas, forsaken by the disciples, condemned by the Jews and crucified by the Romans. You say what has happened to you is unfair? The crucifixion of Jesus was the most unfair event in human history. He allowed them "their hour." Go ahead and take the greatest concentration of evil you can find, bring the full force of death and hell and satan against the Lord Jesus, let evil do all it can do. What is the end result? He is raised up triumphant over it all.

Jesus did not avoid death. Sometimes death is unavoidable. Sometimes darkness is unavoidable. Sometimes evil appears to have the advantage. But in death, in darkness, in the worst evil, Life and Light come forth and God is glorified. If not here where we can see it, then in the End, when all things are revealed, when He makes all things new and wipes away every tear from every eye.

January 8

"Not My will, but Yours, be done."
LUKE 22:42

What does it cost to become a disciple of the Lord Jesus Christ? What does one have to give up? There is truly only one thing that must be given up. It is not, and it never has been, a question of giving up friends, family, material possessions, fame and fortune. You can give up all those things, just like the first disciples of the Lord, and still run away and deny Him.

Forget the outward things and go right to the heart of the matter. Only one thing is necessary, and if we give up this one thing we are qualified to be disciples of the Lord. What is the one thing? All we have to give up is OUR WAY.

There are two ways, one which seems right, and one which IS right. One is my way, the other is His way.

January 9

"You did not choose Me, but I
chose you and appointed you that you
should go and bear fruit, and that your fruit
should remain, that whatever you ask the Father
in My name He may give you."
JOHN 15:16

I t is not so much our seeking the Truth as the
Truth drawing us to Himself. That drawing
us to Himself is interpreted by our soul as
spiritual hunger. Without this we cannot come
to Truth.

Christ has come to seek and to save the Lost.
He tells His disciples that they have not chosen
Him, but He has chosen them. The ones who
seek Him discover that they are sought out by
Him. The paradox of the situation is that the
Lord will only reveal Himself to those who seek
Him, but when they begin to seek Him, He
searches for them in order to make Himself
known.

January 10

"My Father gives you
the True Bread from Heaven."
JOHN 6:32

W hy are we following the Lord? Is it for
what He can do for us? Is it so we can
enjoy His blessing? Is it because He supplies
our needs? Do we want the gifts or the Gift? If
our motivation is for blessings then we will
soon be disappointed. Indeed, from this time
forward, many of His disciples turned back and
stopped following Him. How many of us will
continue to follow when the Lord fails to
respond to us in the way we have grown
accustomed?

The Lord may provide you with bread for a
season, but there is a difference between
looking to the Lord *for* bread and looking to
the Lord *as* bread. May God show us the
difference. The Gift of God is not what Christ
can do for you, but Who He Himself is.

January 11

"Go into all the world and preach
the gospel to every creature."
MARK 16:15

From beginning to end, right up until His ascension, the passionate subject of Jesus Christ was the Kingdom of God. When Jesus finally did send them forth to "go into all the world and preach the Gospel to every creature" this was not a strange new thing for which they were unprepared. They understood (better than ever before) what the Gospel was because Jesus had already given them their mission long before He sent them forth.

It was not just preaching something in a general sort of way and calling it the "Gospel." It was a Kingdom Gospel: "this gospel of the kingdom will be preached in all the world as a witness to all the nations, and then the end will come" (Matthew 24:14).

January 12

"Blessed are you when they revile
and persecute you, and say all kinds of evil
against you falsely for My sake."
MATTHEW 5:11

E xpect misunderstanding. Expect persecution. Expect ridicule. Expect mistreatment. Expect suffering. Expect rejection.
Then, you won't be surprised when it comes.
And when it comes, shut your mouth, go to the
Cross, and die so you can live. Learn to kiss the
hands that nail you to the Cross, for as you are
decreased, He is increased.

It is not a better living we need, but a better
dying. We cannot reach Pentecost but by way of
Passover. There can be no resurrection without
a crucifixion. There is no crown without a
Cross. To live, is Christ: to die is gain.

January 13

"I have been crucified with Christ; it is no longer I who live, but Christ lives in me."
GALATIANS 2:20

P aul says that even though he was crucified, he lives. Does Paul mean to say that he was raised from the dead with Jesus also? If so, why have we not heard about this before now? Finally he says he is not really living at all, but Christ lives in him. To the natural mind, of course, this all sounds very strange. This is why we must discern spiritual things spiritually.

It should be obvious that Paul is talking about something other than a physical crucifixion and a physical death, burial, and resurrection. Although he says, "I was crucified with Christ" he does not mean that he was present with Christ in the flesh at the moment of crucifixion; instead, he intends to show us something much more profound.

We will soon discover that this experience of being crucified with Christ is not unique to the apostle Paul, but is true of every born-again child of God. Not only Paul, but all disciples of Jesus have been crucified with Christ.

January 14

"I, John, both your brother
and companion in the tribulation and
kingdom and patience of Jesus Christ,
was on the island that is called Patmos
for the word of God and for the
testimony of Jesus Christ."
REVELATION 1:9

Since John is an Overcomer, God sends out the call for Overcomers through John. John is symbolic of all Overcomers, and he is the instrument through which God raises up Overcomers.

I can relate to John. I know many of us feel as if we are alone, in exile, in a wilderness. Gradually we feel we are being shut up and shut out by others who have not seen what we have seen. It is right THERE, in the desert place, in the place of exile, in the place of banishment, in the place of dryness, in the place of darkness, that Christ is revealed to us. This ought to encourage us no matter what our situation.

January 15

"The thief does not come except to
steal, and to kill, and to destroy. I have come that
they may have life, and that they may have it
more abundantly."
JOHN 10:10

T hose who hunger and thirst after Righteousness – Christ – will be filled. Thus, the one who is filled is never hungry or thirsty. So on the one hand I want to know the Lord and my desire for Him increases day by day; but it is not the desperate search of a hungry or thirsty man who is fainting and wasting away.

I am full of Him because He fills me. There is my "Life, and Life more abundantly." My Life is not in what He gives me, but in Who He is.

January 16

"Vainly puffed up by his fleshly mind, and not
holding fast to the Head."
COLOSSIANS 2:18,19

Even in the natural realm we know that a healthy physical body does not make decisions or take any action apart from the head. It is the head (i.e., the mind) that determines what the body will do. Indeed, the body cannot properly function apart from the head. When the body is disabled due to injury or disease it means either the body is unable to carry out the instructions of the head or the head is unable to give instructions to the body. We rightly observe this as something that needs medical attention.

Were the head to be separated from the body the result is immediate death. Equally obvious is the fact that the head can take no action without involving the body.

We must not force this metaphor to an extreme and suggest that Jesus is unable to do anything without us; but we can certainly say that Jesus, as the Head of the Ekklesia, will not do anything without involving His Body.

January 17

"And [Jesus] led them out as far as
Bethany, and He lifted up His hands and blessed
them. Now it came to pass, while He blessed
them, that He was parted from them and
carried up into heaven."
LUKE 24:50,51

B ethany has a heavenly savor. There is an ascendant spirit there which lifts us up to the heavenlies. I believe that as we prepare a place for the Lord this ascendant spirit will break forth upon us spontaneously. It is one thing for us to try to act heavenly, and it is quite another thing for us to enter into such communion and fellowship with the Heavenly Man that we simply begin to exude His heavenliness, as the priest in the Holy Place exuded the fragrance of the sweet incense.

The Kingdom of Heaven is where Christ has the preeminence and fills all things: and if this is the case with us individually, or corporately, then it can be said of us that the Kingdom of Heaven has arrived.

January 18

"His feet were like fine brass,
as if refined in a furnace."
REVELATION 1:15

When John was given a revelation of Christ in the Isle of Patmos he described the feet of Jesus as "fine brass as if refined in a furnace." Brass is a symbol of judgment, and the furnace is a symbol of wrath, purification, and refinement. This dimension of the Lord Jesus was something quite new to John.

Because Jesus did not come to judge the world right away, but to save it, we tend to think of Jesus only in terms of the "Lamb" – meek, silent, longsuffering, and turning the other cheek. He certainly is all that.

Yet here we get a glimpse of Jesus as the "Lion." He said He was indeed a King, but that His Kingdom was not of this world. Up until now the kingly aspect of Christ and the majestic glory of His Kingdom had remained hidden.

January 19

"His feet were like burnished bronze,
refined in a furnace... When I saw Him, I fell
at His feet as though dead."
REVELATION 1:15,17 ESV

When this other side of Christ was revealed to John, he "fell at His feet as though dead." At the Last Supper, John had leaned on the Lord's breast and eaten dinner with Him. In this context, however, he can do nothing but collapse at His feet.

There at His feet we discover there is a difference between the Holy and the Human; the One Who comes from Above, and the ones who come from Below; the One Who is Spirit and Truth, and those of us who are merely flesh and blood. His feet are burnished bronze. This is His majesty, and His righteousness. It immediately identifies Him as King of Kings and Lord of Lords, the Righteous Judge, the Living Word Who discerns the thoughts and intents of the heart.

January 20

"We wanted to come to you—even I, Paul,
time and again—but Satan hindered us."
1 THESSALONIANS 2:18

We should not expect things to always go as planned, even when we are indeed following the will of God, and especially when we are trying to do what we feel led to do. Sometimes it seems as if everything is rising up against us. Cars break down, people get sick, misunderstandings arise, businesses fail, things happen.

We do not want to give the devil any glory and attribute everything to him. But we do want to discern the true operation of the enemy so we may dispose of him. We must exercise discernment and wisdom to know the difference between the hand of the Lord, the work of the enemy, and the natural environment. Otherwise we will suffer unnecessarily.

January 21

"He appointed twelve, that they
might be with Him and that He might
send them out to preach..."
MARK 3:14

I like the way Jesus selected His disciples, and the explanation as to why they were selected: "That they might be with Him and that He might send them out to preach" (Mark 3:14). Their being sent forth was contingent upon their having been with the Lord. Preaching was only optional, but being with Him was the primary objective. If they will only be with the Lord then they will have something to say when they do go forth.

January 22

"The gospel which was preached by me
is not according to man. For I neither received
it from man, nor was I taught it, but it came
through the revelation of Jesus Christ."
GALATIANS 1:11,12

With the Biblical record before us, compare what those early disciples believed and preached to what we see and hear being taught and demonstrated in the name of Jesus today. If someone from the apostolic age were to visit our generation, take an account of our lives, document what we preach, and survey what we listen to and currently accept as "The Gospel," how would they respond? Would they be able to say that we preach the Gospel of the Kingdom? Could they report back to their first century friends that we teach the same things they taught concerning the Lord Jesus Christ and the Kingdom of God? Or would they weep and lament at how the Church has distorted the original message of the Ekklesia?

January 23

"As the body is one and has many
members, but all the members of that one body,
being many, are one body, so also is Christ."
1 CORINTHIANS 12:12

The Bible says that there is an invisible but very powerful union that exists between Jesus and all His disciples; they are one Body. It is a spiritual union. This spiritual union forms the basis of our relationship and fellowship with Christ.

Jesus says, "I am the True Vine... Abide in Me, and I in you" (John 15:1,4). Jesus compares this union to a vine that has many branches. Each branch lives in union with the vine. The same life flowing in the vine is also flowing in the branches. Jesus says He is the True Vine, and we are His branches. This is spiritual union. As branches, we can only grow and produce spiritual fruit so long as we continue to live, dwell in, abide, and be part of the Vine. So then, union with God is not the *reward* for spirituality; it is the *basis* of spirituality.

January 24

"Now you are the body of Christ,
and members individually."
1 CORINTHIANS 12:27

There are different members in different places with different purposes: each distinctive but each working together, united beneath the same great Purpose and Intention of God, working under the direction of the Head like a great spiritual symphony.

"God has set the members, each one of them, in the body just as He pleased." (1 Corinthians 12:18). This results in a spiritual oneness and unity (for better or worse) so that "if one member suffers, all the members suffer with it; or if one member is honored, all the members rejoice with it" (1 Corinthians 12:26). Everything you do (or do not do) as a member of the Body of Christ affects all the other members. No one is an island. The Difficult Path may be lonely at times, but we are never truly alone.

January 25

"God... Who desires all men to be saved
and to come to the knowledge of the truth."
1 TIMOTHY 2:4

H ere we see one will of God with two
expressions – a gate and a path. We enter
the gate in a moment, but we walk the path
over time. We are saved in a moment, but we
come to the full-knowledge (epignosis) of
Christ over time. So John 3:3 is not telling us
about our ending, but our beginning. Birth is
the beginning of Life, not the goal of Life. The
goal in view here is not being born-again, but
entering the Kingdom.

Jesus does not just say, "You must be born
again." If He did then we might be correct in
saying that is all there is to it. But Jesus says,
"*Unless* you are born again, you cannot see or
enter into the Kingdom of God." It is clear that
the Kingdom is what we are trying to gain
entrance into, and while being born again is the
gate, the ultimate destination of the Kingdom
of God is at the end of the path.

January 26

"And I will very gladly spend and
be spent for you; though the more abundantly
I love you, the less I am loved."
2 CORINTHIANS 12:15

P aul gave us an example to follow. Don't just look at his calling and his gifting and his revelation. Look at his heart of love. He gave all – not just for the Lord, but for the Lord's people. And they were a most carnal, unappreciative bunch of people. Even so, the heart of a father is demonstrated. That is the reason he had authority. I tell you his authority was not in his title, his position, or his status as having taught the believers there. His authority was not in his calling, gift, or revelation. His authority was in the abundant love he showed.

Make no mistake: I am not there yet. I still struggle with how to be a good brother, much less a spiritual father with abundant love for everyone. I obviously have a long way to go, but now I see the missing ingredient and I am following after Love. How about you?

January 27

"For I determined not
to know anything among you except
Jesus Christ and Him crucified."
1 CORINTHIANS 2:2

Religion seeks to reform a man; the Cross seeks to crucify him. Religion may fail to bring about the desired result, but the Cross never fails to achieve its end.

Mankind will pursue morality, virtue, spirituality, even perform religious works and good deeds, in order to avoid death on a Cross. But there are no wounds, no scars, no evidence of having ever died and been made alive unto God. Either a man has never died, or he has died and been raised again. You cannot fake a resurrection.

January 28

"If you knew the gift of God,
and who it is who says to you, 'Give Me a drink,'
you would have asked Him, and He would
have given you Living Water."
JOHN 4:10

We must know the Gift of God. The one who knows will not only be satisfied, but will have an abundance of Life springing up from within. If we are mainly interested in being filled for ourselves then we will have little to offer anyone else. Yet when we know the Gift of God the Life will overflow. "You anoint my head with oil; my cup runs over" (Psalm 23:5).

Are you an overflowing Christian, with all of God you can hold, and much left over? Sadly, this does not describe many of us. To drink is a beginning, but God's goal is an overflow. How we need clear revelation into the Son! How we need to see just how precious and worthy He is!

January 29

"He who overcomes, and keeps My
works until the end, to him I will give power
over the nations—*'He shall rule them with a rod
of iron; they shall be dashed to pieces like the
potter's vessels'*— as I also have received
from My Father; and I will give
him the morning star."
REVELATION 2:26-28

J ust as Jeremiah was set over nations and kingdoms, so we have received this authority also. We do not serve in a governmental capacity, but in a spiritual capacity, praying for the Kingdom and Will of God to come forth. Such prayer is very weighty and universal. It is beyond the earth, and so it moves the earth.

In addition to authority over the nations, we are given "the morning star." Christ is the Morning Star, the Heavenly Man, Who is higher than the nations and kingdoms of this world. The Morning Star gives Overcomers the heavenly authority which is beyond the influence of the earthly realm in which they must live.

January 30

"Little children, keep yourselves from
idols (false gods)—[from anything and everything
that would occupy the place in your heart due to
God, from any sort of substitute for Him that
would take first place in your life]."
1 JOHN 5:21 AMP

T hat is the sort of radical, uncompromising attitude he says we must exercise over our own hearts, for as the members go, so goes the whole Body. Just look at the gravity of his words! "Keep yourself from ANYTHING and EVERYTHING that would occupy the place in your heart due to God, from ANY SORT of substitute for Him that would take first place in your life." Fanatical, impossible directions! Do you really mean to say that there can be NOTHING that takes first place in my life but Christ? Is that what it comes down to?

Absolutely, that is precisely what is at stake, and that is precisely where the battle rages, and that is precisely why we are being tempted on a daily basis. All we have to do to be defeated is to put Him some place other than first. Either He is Lord OF all, or He is not Lord AT all.

January 31

"Of His fullness we have all received."
JOHN 1:16

I f there is a seeming difference in the "level" of anointing or power or spirituality among believers it is definitely not because some have more of the Lord than others. Let this be an encouragement to you. Indeed, Christ is not divided, and of His fullness we all share. We are all baptized into the same Spirit.

The difference is some saints are more broken than others. Some have passed through many seasons of tearing down and building up, while some after many years of experience are still resisting the Lord and refusing to lay down their lives. Some have recognized God's dealings and have submitted to them, while others have misunderstood or been totally ignorant of God's dealings with them.

February 1

"Yours is the Kingdom, and the
Power, and the Glory forever. Amen."
MATTHEW 6:13

What assurance are we given? It is this: that in spite of nation rising up against nation, kingdom rising up against kingdom, political tumults and global confusion, "YOURS IS THE KINGDOM" – Your Throne is everlasting, Your Kingdom is established, and of the increase of Your Government there shall be no end (Isaiah 9:6,7).

In other words, as Daniel would say, the Heavens DO rule, and it is the Most High God Who governs the affairs of men. THAT is the heart of the matter. THAT is what we are moving towards, from our day-to-day affairs as followers of Jesus, to the course and direction of this entire age.

February 2

"That which is born of the flesh is flesh,
and that which is born of the Spirit is spirit.
Do not marvel that I said to you,
'You must be born again.'"
JOHN 3:6,7

Jesus said that to see His Kingdom "you must be born-again." To enter His Kingdom, He requires us to "become as little children" (Matthew 18:3).

That is another way of saying, "You have to start all over again. You cannot make any progress with Me so long as you cling to the old way of thinking, perceiving, understanding, and interacting. I cannot pour new wine into old wineskins because it would ruin both. You need a new wineskin — a new heart, a new mind, a new understanding of things in order to receive what I wish to give you."

February 3

"He who is joined to the
Lord is one spirit with Him."
1 CORINTHIANS 6:17

To the Ephesians, Paul compares this spiritual union to the union that exists between a man and a woman when they are married: "And the two shall become one flesh. This is a great mystery, but I speak concerning Christ and the [Ekklesia]" (Ephesians 5:31,32). Certainly this is a great mystery.

How God is able to make us one spirit with Jesus is beyond human knowledge. But this we know: however it is accomplished, it has its beginning in the Cross. The Cross is the starting point of our union with Christ. In the Cross, God sees us in the place of Christ and sees Christ in the place of us. That is to say, in the Cross, all our sinfulness is attributed to Christ, and all His righteousness is attributed to us. How wonderful for us – but how terrible for Him!

February 4

"What things were gain to me,
these I have counted loss for Christ. Yet
indeed I also count all things loss for the
excellence of the knowledge of Christ Jesus
my Lord, for whom I have suffered the loss
of all things, and count them as rubbish,
that I may gain Christ."
PHILIPPIANS 3:7,8

The ones who have been sufficiently broken eventually manifest very little of their self, and very much of Christ. God must work long and hard with us to bring us to this place, but what a glorious day it is when we are able to bow our heads and finally surrender everything.

What joy it is to look back over all that the Lord has led us through and realize His purpose in both the good times and the bad times, to behold the goodness and the severity of God in His dealings with us.

February 5

"Because of Him you are in Christ Jesus, who
became to us wisdom from God, righteousness
and sanctification and redemption."
1 CORINTHIANS 1:30 ESV

H ave you ever seen a brother or a sister try
to act sanctified? They wear themselves
and everyone else out. It is a burden to be
around such a person. That is not Christianity.

Christianity is this: not that I am trying to be
wise, but that I receive the Lord Jesus as my
Wisdom; not that I am trying to be righteous,
but that I receive the Lord Jesus as my
Righteousness; not that I am trying to be
sanctified, but that I receive the Lord Jesus as
my Sanctification; not that I am trying to be
redeemed, but that I accept the Lord Jesus as
my Redemption. Henceforth I cease trying to
be anything, and I allow Him to be Who He is
through me.

February 6

"A woman came to Him having
an alabaster flask of very costly fragrant oil,
and she poured it on His head as He sat at the
table. But when His disciples saw it, they
were indignant, saying, 'Why this waste?
For this fragrant oil might have been sold
for much and given to the poor.'"
MATTHEW 26:7-9

We want to appear to be busy doing for God, busy at our "ministry." But there is a place where we simply "waste" ourselves on Him, and outwardly we appear to be doing nothing.

Would that more believers would "waste" themselves more often, ministering to the Lord, sitting at His feet, hearing His word, ministering to Him in secret prayer and fasting! Then when they do rise up to work, how much more fruitful they will be!

February 7

"I fear, lest somehow, as the
serpent deceived Eve by his craftiness, so
your minds may be corrupted from the
simplicity that is in Christ."
2 CORINTHIANS 11:3

I have said many times that we do not need more of the Lord, since we are already complete in Christ – we just need less of everything else. There are many things that spoil, hinder, distract, and lead us away from the simplicity of an abiding relationship with Jesus. Many of them are spiritual and religious. The spirit of Antichrist is not necessarily seen in something that is obviously satanic or demonic. Instead, the spirit of Antichrist is revealed in anything that seeks to spoil us by taking our eyes off of Christ – it is anti-Christ, against Christ, antithetical to the great Purpose of God.

How easy it is for us to become distracted into something less than Christ! Are you centered on Christ? Is Jesus your obsession? Is He your focus? Or have you set your sights on something beneath Him?

February 8

"Put on the Lord Jesus Christ, and make
no provision for the flesh, to fulfill its lusts."
ROMANS 13:14

God's Solution to the problem of sin, self, and satan is to have us put on the Lord Jesus. Only through Him can we "make no provision for the flesh," and only through Him can we "stand against the wiles of the devil." We dare not make it more complicated when the Lord has made it simple.

To focus on our flesh and on our enemy is a huge waste of time. Instead, we must perceive just how glorious the Son of God is, and press deeply into Him. Do you have a method, or a Man? It is not about me, my flesh, or the devil – it is all about Christ, and as He is increased, none of these other things can do anything but be decreased.

February 9

"Far be it from You, Lord;
this shall not happen to You!"
MATTHEW 16:22

See how many times the disciples tried to correct the Lord. See how many times they argued with the Lord. See how many times their thoughts contradicted the Master. See how many times they urged Him to take action. And the Lord, ever patient, would correct them.

In every case we see that He is the Lord, and they are the disciples. The roles must never be confused. He is the Master, and we are His servants. We do not command Him, but He commands us. We do not lead Him, but He leads us. He was not created for us, but we were created for Him. He does not serve us according to our pleasure, but we serve Him according to His pleasure. So we must be adjusted to Him, and not the other way around. The Lord will never apologize to us and say, "I'm sorry, I was wrong. We'll do it your way." How laughable! How absurd! But we often live as if we expect Him to do that very thing. We have not humbled ourselves.

February 10

"There was an army, surrounding
the city with horses and chariots. And his servant
said to him, 'Alas, my master! What shall we do?'
So he answered, 'Do not fear, for those who are
with us are more than those who are with them.'
And Elisha prayed, and said, 'Lord, I pray, open
his eyes that he may see.' Then the Lord opened
the eyes of the young man, and he saw."
2 KINGS 6:15-17

When the servant's eyes were opened, he saw what Elisha saw. When Elisha said, "Those who are with us are more than those who are with them" it must have sounded like lunacy. It cannot be understood with words alone: the eyes must be opened. If words were enough then Elisha would not have prayed for the eyes to be opened.

We should spend less time trying to understand "words" and more time praying for God to open our eyes. When our eyes are opened, then the words will make sense. Until then, words are like hieroglyphics – we know there is something significant there, but we cannot understand what it means.

February 11

"The mystery which has been hidden
from ages and from generations, but now has
been revealed to His saints. To them God willed
to make known what are the riches of the glory
of this mystery among the Gentiles: which is
Christ in you, the hope of glory."
COLOSSIANS 1:26,27

Here is an amazing fact: the Bible says that we carry this Treasure (Jesus) within earthen vessels. In other words, the Living Christ indwells us now. We are His House, His Temple, His Dwelling Place, His Body.

I doubt if we really comprehend that. Do we really know that we are in Him, and He is in us?

February 12

"He made Him who knew no sin
to be sin for us, that we might become
the righteousness of God in Him."
2 CORINTHIANS 5:21

When we submit to the Cross, God identifies us with Christ just the same as if we were sinless. Jesus becomes our wisdom, righteousness, sanctification, and redemption (1 Corinthians 1:30). It does not say that He gives these things to us, it says He *is* these things to us.

Was Jesus crucified for His sins? No, He was crucified for our sins. Are we now wise, righteous, sanctified, and redeemed because of anything we have done? No, God simply identifies us together with Christ, as if we were crucified together with Him. He loses everything and we gain everything. This is why salvation begins with repentance, surrender, and faith in Christ and His finished work on the Cross. It cannot be accomplished otherwise. What a glorious Lord we have!

February 13

"[Abraham] was looking forward
to the city that has foundations, whose
designer and builder is God."
HEBREWS 11:10 ESV

An artist sees a new painting before he picks up the brush to create it. A musician hears a new song in her head before she picks up her instrument to compose it. A writer conceives ideas, concepts, and things to be conveyed to others in his heart long before he sets words to paper. An architect designs the building before construction begins.

The creative process is the progressive, orderly arrangement of things until what is seen outwardly lines up with what has already been seen inwardly. God is the Ultimate Creator. We find that He established an order of things before He ever brought them into being – an eternal purpose that He purposed in Christ. The crucifixion of Christ was not God's startled reaction to the unforeseen and unimaginable fall of Adam. God envisioned things straight through to the end before He set them in motion.

February 14

"Do you also want to go away?"
JOHN 6:67

J esus sought to thin out the crowds with a difficult word, saying, "You must eat My flesh and drink My blood if you wish to be My disciples." At this saying, the multitude and many of His disciples turned aside and no longer followed Him. Instead of running after them in an effort to make Himself understood and accepted, He watched them go. Then, turning to the Twelve, He said, "Do you also want to go away?" Here is a Man who is not afraid to be misunderstood because He is not afraid of people, what they will think, or what they will say about Him unjustly.

To overcome the fear of man, we must not only be willing to be misunderstood and unappreciated, we should expect it. Then we will be free to speak what God has given us and will not be troubled should others fail to grasp the significance of it.

February 15

"Whom are you seeking?"
JOHN 18:4

In other words, who are you looking for? This particular crowd was pressing in to have Jesus arrested and put to death. The day before the crowds were pressing in to proclaim "Hosanna!", and before that they were pressing in to make Him their king by force (John 6:15). At other times the people pressed Him to hear the Word of God. Still other times the people pressed Him to be healed of their diseases.

Pressing Him, pushing Him, forever wanting more and never satisfied. Very few know how to sit at His feet just to hear His Word. Very few are willing to pour out the best ointment on Him, and when they do, they are severely criticized for such a "waste."

Does anyone seek Him for His sake? Does anyone press upon Him, not for what He can give, but for Who He is? Does anyone seek Him out, not to get some need met, but so they "may know Him" (Philippians 3:10)?

February 16

"Commit your way to the Lord, trust also
in Him, and He shall bring it to pass."
PSALM 37:5

We want the Lord's Life, but we also want to retain a little something of our life. That will never work. This is why you have such ups and downs, simply because you still love your life, and only trust in His Life for the really difficult moments. In a bad situation you will throw yourself upon His Life and it will carry you on through, but in the normal everyday situations you live according to your own life.

Instead, let us learn to trust in His Life for every moment of every day. If we will surrender everything His Life will reproduce in us more effectively, gradually transforming, renewing, invigorating, and sustaining us from the inside out.

February 17

"Blessed are the poor in spirit, for
theirs is the Kingdom of Heaven."
MATTHEW 5:3

T his spiritual poverty is the result of recognizing that apart from Him we can do nothing. It is a willingness to be broken and reduced to spiritual bankruptcy, which implies not only losing everything we once enjoyed, but also making a fresh start with a clean slate and all our debts erased. It is the Second Universal Spiritual Principle, which states: "I must decrease" (John 3:30). This decreasing, or as I like to say, this reducing to Christ, is the first requirement.

If we are unwilling to be emptied then we cannot have the riches of the Kingdom of Heaven. We will be like the Laodicean church, who said they were "rich and increased with goods and have need of nothing" yet in God's sight they were poor, blind, naked, and miserable (Revelation 3:17). So the Kingdom belongs to those who readily admit right from the beginning that "a man can receive nothing unless it has been given to him from heaven " (John 3:27).

February 18

"He who comes from above is
above all; he who is of the earth is earthly
and speaks of the earth. He who comes
from heaven is above all."
JOHN 3:31

If people come against you in the flesh, let them come against you. If they wish to rail and argue with you according to the flesh, do not respond in kind. If they attack you without cause, let them attack, because the fleshly, the carnal, the natural cannot defeat the spiritual.

The one who is submitted to the Lord has authority over those who remain unsubmitted to Him. Flesh is overruled by Spirit. Hate is overruled by Love. Darkness is overruled by Light. Death is overruled by Life. Earth is overruled by Heaven.

February 19

"Rise and stand on your feet; for
I have appeared to you for this purpose…"
ACTS 26:16

The Lord has a purpose for you, and a destiny for you to fulfill. But things will not always go the way you think they should. That is because the Lord calls you to something bigger than yourself, something beyond your ability, something you cannot originate or perpetuate without Him. It takes time. Noah walked with God for five hundred years and spent one hundred years building the ark. Abraham was one hundred years old before he finally saw God's promise come true. Moses spent forty years in Egypt, then forty years in the desert, before God sent him to Pharaoh. Jesus prepared thirty years for an earthly ministry of three and a half years.

Dear brother, dear sister: walk with God. Find Grace. Discover the One Thing. Focus on being, not doing. And when it IS time for you to do something you can be confident that your labor of love will be the work that God blesses.

February 20

"I can do all things through
Christ who strengthens me."
PHILIPPIANS 4:13

We don't have to imitate His Life, we only have to trust His Life! Trust in His Life to do it in, through, and on behalf of us who cannot do it! If you have ever once trusted in His Life to keep you from losing your temper, you can trust in His Life every single time you are confronted with it, and He will bring you through. Without exception. Along those lines, I can say with all confidence, that if you can trust His Life to overwhelm your temper, you can trust His Life for everything else. What do you need? Do you worry too much? Are you fearful? Are you bitter? His Life indwells you right now, and longs to make you into something totally new, to transfigure you into something entirely different than what you are now. Thank the Lord that I don't have to be the way I am, but there is hope for me, and there is hope for you, and there is hope for the worst sinner on the face of the earth, because it is not a question of my effort, but of His sufficiency!

February 21

"You also have become dead to
the law through the body of Christ, that you
may be married to another—to Him who was
raised from the dead, that we should
bear fruit to God."
ROMANS 7:4

Y ou may wonder how this union with Jesus was accomplished. I do not have the answer to that, but I consider it to be so because God says it is so. God placed us in Christ. I do not fully understand how He did this, but I know that He did it, and I thank God for it. The Bible says that "because of [God] you are in Christ Jesus" (1 Corinthians 1:30).

Disciples of Jesus are one with Christ because God has placed us there. We are in Christ, and Christ is in us. We may not understand how this can be so, but it is so. We are spiritually one with Christ. This oneness, this union, this partnership and fellowship with Him is the basis of our spiritual life and our walk with God.

February 22

"Where is your faith?"
LUKE 8:25

What is faith? Is it a spiritual force? Is it a creative power? Is it a special gift from God, or something we have to develop on our own? According to the Bible, faith is simply believing that God is Who He says He is, and trusting that He will do what He says He will do. When Jesus says, "Where is your faith?" He's saying, "Don't you trust Me?"

I'm convinced that we have plenty of faith. The problem is we have faith in all the wrong things. Where is your faith? In yourself? In other people? Can you only trust what you see, hear, and experience, or will you dare to trust Someone you can't see? Believing the impossible makes the impossible possible.

February 23

"God has set the members, each one of
them, in the body just as He pleased."
1 CORINTHIANS 12:18

A Christian should realize that he or she is a unique member of the Body of Christ and not the entire Body all at once. We are many parts that together make up the whole. Each individual member has its own unique purpose, function, and role. The responsibility for God's work is divided among many members.

We are not called to be all things to all people. We are not called to meet every need. God sets each person in the Body of Christ as it pleases Him, and He is the One Who sends us. We do not send ourselves. We do not determine what we would like to do. We do not analyze the situation with our limited understanding and come up with a solution. The Head determines what needs to be done, and the members simply perform it.

February 24

"In the beginning was the Word,
and the Word was with God, and the Word was
God. He was in the beginning with God."
JOHN 1:1,2

When you read the first chapter of John's gospel you discover the presence of Someone Who "in the beginning" was with God and was God at the same time. We will not attempt to explain the unexplainable; suffice it to say, the Word that was with God, and was God, and eventually "became flesh and dwelt among us" (John 1:14) is the Lord Jesus Christ.

When God created man, it says He breathed the breath of life into him (Genesis 2:7). Here, John states that the Light (Jesus Christ) is the Life of men. What is the point? That before anything was created, God determined in advance that the universe, and everything in it, would be established, presided over, and governed by, through, and for Jesus Christ – and God has never altered from that original intention and purpose. This forms the basic principle of the Heavenly Order, which in turn governs the Irresistible Kingdom.

February 25

"Then these men assembled,
and found Daniel praying and making
supplication before his God."
DANIEL 6:11

S omething should be driving us to pray. There should be some unction, some inner compulsion, to seek God, to seek Him early, and to seek Him often. If that is not our daily experience then something is wrong.

Perhaps we have grown complacent, or comfortable, or cold. Whatever the reason, vision is the cure. If we have truly seen God's Purpose we cannot just go along as before. It will consume us. A person with a small vision will pray small prayers. Daniel was a man of huge vision, and so he prayed large prayers.

February 26

"As newborn babes, desire
the pure milk of the Word, that you
may grow thereby."
1 PETER 2:2

When we realize we don't know, then Christ becomes our Wisdom so we CAN know.

When we are children we are apt to say, I know WHAT I believe. As we grow out of infancy and begin to wrestle with the deeper questions and issues of the Christian faith we will learn to say, I know WHY I believe. The ultimate experience, however, is to be brought to a place where we can say with confidence, I know WHOM I believe.

Knowing WHAT is a beginning.

Knowing WHY is progress.

Knowing WHO is maturity.

February 27

"Let that abide in you which you heard
from the beginning. If what you heard from the
beginning abides in you, you also will abide in
the Son and in the Father."
1 JOHN 2:24

There is still much of Him to learn and to experience. There is much growing which must take place. The Path is a process. We are hardly ever as far along as we imagine ourselves to be. But we have not been talking about spiritual maturity, but spiritual satisfaction. If, in abiding continually in the Lord, He becomes our food and our drink, then we will grow.

Growth is not the result of time, it is the natural result of Christ increasing and us decreasing. The Law of Life says that Christ must increase. Now we can do nothing to speed up this process, but we can certainly hinder or quench it.

February 28

"Father, into Your hands I commit My spirit."
LUKE 23:46

Death by crucifixion cannot be accomplished by suicide. We cannot crucify ourselves.

The instrument of our death is chosen for us, as well as the manner in which it is carried out, the timing, and the duration of the execution – all is controlled by Another. There is nothing to be done, for we must submit to the Unseen Hand and cast ourselves completely upon Him.

February 29

"These who have turned the world
upside down have come here too."
ACTS 17:6

If God can find a man or a woman who will give Him the preeminence and will give Him the freedom to increase, then there is no limit to what God can do through that yielded vessel. And if He can find a handful of people like that then He will use them to turn the world upside down. It has happened once before and I am positive that it can happen again.

The Father is seeking those who will worship Him in Spirit and in TRUTH. Has He found what He is looking for in you? Will you be the one? Will you be the chosen?

March 1

"If anyone is in Christ, he is a
new creation; old things have passed away;
behold, all things have become new."
2 CORINTHIANS 5:17

When God placed us in Christ, He forever linked us to Christ's death, burial, resurrection, ascension, and being seated in the heavenlies. So God considers us to have been crucified, dead, buried, resurrected, ascended, and seated as well. It cannot be otherwise. So long as we remain in Him (John 15:5) our destinies are linked.

I once placed a $20 bill inside of a book. I then misplaced the book. What happened to the $20 bill? The bill was lost when the book was lost. The bill and the book were linked together because I placed one inside the other. In order to find the bill I had to find the book. Once I found the book, I also found the bill. In like manner, God has placed us in Christ. When Christ was crucified, we were also crucified. When Christ was raised, we were also raised. The two have become one, and what is true of Him is true of all those who are one with Him.

March 2

"Paul dwelt two whole years in his
own rented house, and received all who came to
him, preaching the kingdom of God and teaching
the things which concern the Lord Jesus Christ
with all confidence, no one forbidding him."
ACTS 28:30,31

A postles, prophets, evangelists, pastors and teachers must point people to Christ. Otherwise they are not fulfilling the purpose for which God placed them in the Body to begin with. Apostolic ministry is not an end unto itself, but is a means to an end. Prophetic ministry is not an end unto itself, but is a means to an end. Evangelistic ministry is not an end unto itself, but is a means to an end. Pastoral and teaching ministries are not ends unto themselves, but are a means to an end.

What is the end? What is the purpose? What does it all lead to? It leads to "the measure of the stature of the fullness of Christ" (Ephesians 4:13). The fullness of Christ, the full-knowledge of Him – this is God's Goal and His Ultimate Intention.

March 3

"And they overcame him by the blood
of the Lamb and by the word of their testimony,
and they did not love their lives to the death."
REVELATION 12:11

It is helpful to identify the three enemies that present themselves to us, and then the above verse will make even more sense. The overcomer must learn how to defeat each one. So what are they?

First, there is the enemy of Sin. Second, the enemy of Self. Third, the enemy of Satan. All contrary things, whether they be of spiritual, natural, or human origin, find their root in one of these three sources.

The glorious thing, of course, is that God's provision meets all three enemies and defeats them in order to demonstrate the preeminence of Christ. This, in essence, is what it means to overcome. It is to demonstrate the preeminence of Christ over all things.

March 4

"But of Him you are in Christ Jesus,
who became for us wisdom from God—
and righteousness and sanctification and
redemption—that, as it is written, 'He
who glories, let him glory in the Lord.'"
1 CORINTHIANS 1:30,31

We must be clear: these things are not the "reward" for years of faithful service, or the fruit of walking with Jesus after a long period of time. If I have Him now, then I have all that pertains to Him now. My Wisdom, my Righteousness, my Sanctification, and my Redemption has a personality, for He is all those things in me.

It is not a question of my behavior, or my conduct, or my feelings one way or the other – those things will come into line soon enough – but it is all based upon this accomplished fact. Christ is God's Gift. I repeat, we have much to praise God about!

March 5

"I, if I am lifted up from the earth, will
draw all peoples to Myself."
JOHN 12:32

The increase of Christ does not coerce, it compels; He does not push, He merely draws. The increase of Christ actually enables a person to choose the right way, the way that leads to Life. It is evil that deceives people into choosing the wrong path. Everyone born into this world comes into it as a fallen creature. If they had a full understanding of their spiritual condition, and the deliverance that is offered by and through the Lord Jesus, then they would, of course, choose to be delivered.

People only resist what they do not know and understand. Jesus does not have to manipulate anyone. Once a person with eyes wide open sees Him for Who He is, they will always choose Him. He is irresistible. And as He increases, as He is lifted up, He will draw all men unto Himself.

March 6

"Peter remembered the word of
Jesus who had said to him, 'Before the
rooster crows, you will deny Me three times.'
So he went out and wept bitterly."
MATTHEW 26:75

Jesus was not surprised or disappointed when Peter failed. In like manner, He is not surprised or disappointed when you fail. Rather, He is waiting for you to fail so you will be reduced to Him. He has no illusions about you and He knows you through and through. He knows however much your spirit may be willing, your flesh is weak. Our weakness is not the trouble – the trouble is our unwillingness to acknowledge the weakness.

But I bring you good tidings of great joy, dear Christian friend! This failure of Self is the very key to living the Christian life. As painful as it is, the bitter tears of failure provide the water for nurturing the Precious Seed that is planted in your heart of hearts and making it grow. To despair of ourselves is the very key that opens the door to all the power, the victory, and fruitfulness in Christ that we seek.

March 7

"You are complete in Him."
COLOSSIANS 2:10

The truth is that you are no more complete in Him today than you were when you first received Him, however long ago that may have been. And you will never be any more complete in Him than you are right now. You are complete in Him – of course, in yourself, you are far from complete, but that is not the issue. "In me" I am growing, learning, struggling, and maturing. But the issue is not "me." The issue is, "not I, but Christ."

With less of me, there is more of Him. That is why we say that true spiritual growth is not more knowledge or increase of years. It is simply more of Christ and less of me. This is only the decreasing of Self which makes way for the increasing of Christ (John 3:30). Eventually we will view every weakness of ours as an opportunity to see Christ revealed as Strength. Every momentary "lack" is an opportunity to see Christ as Infinite Supply. For this is the Will and Purpose of God: that Christ may be All in All.

March 8

"Unless you eat the flesh of
the Son of Man and drink His blood, you
do not have life in you [Gate]... Whoever
continues to eat my flesh and drink my blood
continues to live in union with Me and I in
union with him [Path]."
JOHN 6:53,56 (Williams)

My burden is to see disciples brought down the Path, so I see the Path everywhere I look in the Scripture. How does this relate to our study? In this way: the Gate of eternal Life is to receive the Lord as food and drink, but the Path is to continue eating and drinking.

The Lord tells us that He is meat indeed, and drink indeed. Just how often do we eat and drink? Unless we are fasting, our eating and drinking occur daily, several times a day in fact. That is why I selected the Williams Translation of these passages, because it gives us the continuing action of the Greek verb – whoever *continues* to eat, *continues* to live. It is not just a once-and-for-all thing, but a continual thing. It is abiding. It is a Gate and a Path.

March 9

"I am the bread of life. He who comes
to Me shall never hunger, and he who believes
in Me shall never thirst."
JOHN 6:35

H ere we have another principle of how the Law of Life operates. The presence of this Life within the believer will create hunger and thirst for Christ. What is more, this hunger and thirst for Christ cannot be filled or quenched with anything else – including blessings, power, spiritual gifts, or Christian service.

It is hard to convince new converts of this, but those of us who have been around a long time should know by now that Christ is what makes a Christian.

March 10

"In Him we live, move and have our being."
ACTS 17:28

Before my father married my mother and conceived me, he was in a serious automobile accident. Had my father died at the age of sixteen, I would have died also, because I was still in my father. His death would have been my death; and not my death only, but also the death of my children, and their children, all the way down the line. We would have all died together with him, having never even lived. But his life, his survival, his overcoming the accident was just as much my life, my survival, and my overcoming.

Spiritually speaking, this is similar to what God has done for us by placing us in Christ. Christ was crucified, dead, buried, resurrected, ascended, and seated; and since we were in Him when it all happened, God considers it to have happened to us as well. We who are His children now share in the very life of Christ, and each of us bear witness to the resurrection and overcoming of Christ. When God raised Him from the dead, He raised us from the dead as well.

March 11

"I have heard of You by the hearing
of the ear, but now my eye sees You. Therefore I
abhor myself and repent in dust and ashes."
JOB 42:5,6

Hearing about God from others is not the same as seeing Him with your own eyes. In Job's story we find an answer to the age-old question of why God allows the righteous to suffer. The answer is: there are things you need to know about God, and things you need to know about yourself, that you cannot know without going through a fiery trial.

The greatest lessons will not be learned while sitting in a classroom or reading a book. They will be learned in the dark nights, the deep valleys, and the raging seas of trial and tribulation.

March 12

"And [Jesus] entered a house and wanted
no one to know it, but He could not be hidden."
MARK 7:24

When we look at the earthly ministry of Jesus we see that He did not seek to increase Himself. He actually humbled Himself and tried to be inconspicuous. Even so, when He tried to hide Himself, He could not be hidden. I want you to think about that. When God was ready to reveal Him then He could not be hidden. He could not even hide Himself.

I tell you, this idea of Christ increasing is the most powerful reality in this universe! Nothing can stand before it, nothing can resist it, and nothing can stop it.

March 13

"When I broke the five loaves
for the five thousand, how many baskets
full of fragments did you take up? ...Also, when I
broke the seven for the four thousand, how
many large baskets full of fragments
did you take up?"
MARK 8:19,20

When you're going through a crisis of faith, it's not easy to remember the faithfulness of the Lord. How quickly we forget the previous victories and the former blessings.

Jesus wants us to remember. Keeping a spiritual journal or prayer diary is a good way to remember just how far the Lord has brought us and just how much He has done for us. Our circumstances may change, but He never changes! He is always faithful.

Remember the loaves and do the math, Jesus says. When you do, you will see this simple truth: the fewer loaves you start out with, the more people I can feed. My Power is strongest when you are at your weakest.

March 14

"The Law of the Spirit of Life in Christ Jesus has
made me free from the Law of Sin and Death."
ROMANS 8:2

Does a fish become a fish by swimming under the water, or does it swim under the water because it is a fish? Does a bird become a bird once it learns to fly through the air? Or does it fly through the air because it is a bird? Which is it? Of course, the bird is a bird, and therefore it flies. It does not have to be instructed per se, but when it is pushed out of the nest it flaps its wings. It is its nature to do so. So doing does not create being, doing flows out of being.

Now the Law of Life in Christ does not try to make us into something we are not. The very presence of the Life in us demonstrates that Christ already indwells us. We are not trying to be like Christ, and we are not trying to live like a Christian. Since we ARE in Him, we WALK in Him. Our works come from what we are, not what we are trying to be.

March 15

> "God also has highly exalted Him and
> given Him the name which is above every name,
> that at the name of Jesus every knee should bow,
> of those in heaven, and of those on earth, and
> of those under the earth, and that every
> tongue should confess that Jesus Christ is
> Lord, to the glory of God the Father."
> PHILIPPIANS 2:9-11

Christ will have the preeminence in all things, but it will not be the forced submission of a dictator who forces everyone to bow down to him whether they want to or not. It is true that some seem to bow down more easily than others; some are quick to confess Jesus as Lord, others confess Him as Lord when they are older, while some seem to hold out until the last possible moment. Some apparently die having made no obvious confession of faith at all.

But in the end, we have the glorious promise. Note how Scripture includes "every tongue" and "every knee." The Bible affirms that "He is able even to subdue all things unto Himself" (Philippians 3:21).

March 16

"I say to you, that unless your
righteousness exceeds the righteousness of
the scribes and Pharisees, you will by no means
enter the kingdom of heaven."
MATTHEW 5:20

We know we must leave sin because we can appreciate how horrible it is. We do not so quickly leave "our righteousness" because we think somehow it has been "purified."

Mark well, however, that God does not fix the old man, but destroys it. He does not tell us to clean up our life, but to lay down our life. It is not enough to forsake the wrong: we must allow Him to crucify the right. That is, we must learn to hate our thoughts that we may have His mind. We must give up our "spiritual" desires in order to have Christ as All.

March 17

"If anyone desires to come after Me,
let him deny himself, and take up his cross
daily, and follow Me."
LUKE 9:23

When we first come to the Lord we truly think we are giving Him our all, but we cannot fully appreciate just how powerful Self is. It cannot be dealt with in a once-and-for-all manner. It requires many seasons of God's dealings for us to see the truth about the Lord, and the truth about ourselves.

That is why I say there is more hope for someone who is ready to give up and quit than there is for someone who keeps promising to do better tomorrow. Only after we have tried and failed one hundred, one thousand, or one million times will we at last be able to say, "Lord, I finally understand now that I can originate nothing of my own self, because whenever I do, I meet with nothing but defeat. So I am finished! Henceforth, not my will, but Your Will be done!"

March 18

"God forbid that I should boast
except in the cross of our Lord Jesus
Christ, by whom the world has been crucified
to me, and I to the world."
GALATIANS 6:14

Whereas the Holy Spirit is instrumental in the increase of Christ, the Cross is instrumental in the decrease of Self. Remember that the whole trouble with man is his inherent tendency to travel a path that is independent of his Creator. This is why the Cross must do a very deep, thorough work in every disciple of Jesus.

As Self is submitted to Christ, Sin begins to lose its power of attraction, and Satan has no more leverage. The night He was betrayed, Jesus told His disciples, "The ruler of this world is coming, and he has nothing in Me" (John 14:30). That is to say, there was nothing in the Lord Jesus that the devil could use to get an advantage over Him. This is the condition He desires for each of His disciples, and the Cross is the means through which that condition is arrived at.

March 19

"Beware lest anyone cheat you
through philosophy and empty deceit,
according to the tradition of men, according
to the basic principles of the world, and
not according to Christ."
COLOSSIANS 2:8

How can we be cheated? According to Paul we are cheated "through philosophy and empty deceit, according to the tradition of men, according to the basic principles (elements) of the world, and not according to Christ."

It matters not if the philosophy is good, right, morally excellent, and praiseworthy. It matters not how well intentioned, meaningful, or helpful the tradition is. It matters not how necessary we think the worldly element to be, or how important it is to society in general. If none of these things are "according to Christ," that is, if they are not of Him, through Him, and unto Him, then they are worthless insofar as God's Purpose is concerned and must be discarded.

March 20

"Those who are Christ's have crucified
the flesh with its passions and desires."
GALATIANS 5:24

Scripture says that those who belong to Christ Jesus have crucified (past tense) the flesh with its passions and desires. No one can commit suicide by crucifixion. Someone else must nail us to the Cross. The flesh cannot crucify itself. Jesus has already done what we could not do. The sooner we stop trying to crucify ourselves, the sooner we can boast in the finished work of the Cross and actually witness the evidence of it in our lives.

Notice that Paul does not merely say that Jesus was crucified for us. That is certainly true in and of itself. But there is more. Not only was Jesus crucified *for* us, He was crucified *as* us. God considers us to have been crucified as surely as if we were there receiving the nails in our hands and feet. We have been crucified together with Him because God placed us in Him the moment He was crucified.

March 21

"We do not yet see all things
put under Him. But we see Jesus... for Whom
are all things and by Whom are all things."
HEBREWS 2:8-10

Do we see it yet? Not in its fullness, no. We have a little here, and a little there. Where this has already happened, where we actually see and experience Christ having the preeminence, it is called the Kingdom of God. It is not a visible thing, but an invisible thing, for Jesus said the Kingdom is not seen, but is within you.

Eventually the Kingdom of God will swallow up the entire Creation and Christ will have the preeminence in all things. Why? Because all things are for Him, and all things were by Him.

March 22

"The Helper, the Holy Spirit, whom
the Father will send in My name, He will teach
you all things, and bring to your remembrance
all things that I said to you."
JOHN 14:26

The Holy Spirit is the vessel – the Person, the instrument, the agency, the method and the means – through Whom God accomplishes His purpose of increasing Christ in all things. Jesus said this Helper, this Counselor, this Comforter, this Teacher will abide with us for– ever and will help us as we walk the Difficult Path towards the full knowledge of Christ.

To the extent that we allow ourselves to come under the government of the Holy Spirit, to that extent will Christ be increased. Since the Holy Spirit is responsible for the increase of Christ, spiritual growth is impossible apart from the Spirit. There will be no measurable advancement, no real apprehension of spiritual things, and no recovery of the Heavenly Order apart from the ministry of the Holy Spirit.

March 23

"It is done! I am the Alpha and the
Omega, the Beginning and the End.
I will give of the fountain of the water of Life
freely to him who thirsts. He who overcomes
shall inherit all things, and I will be his God
and he shall be My son."
REVELATION 21:6,7

As we look at the promises made to those who overcome we should see that God is not establishing some new order or special group which enjoys rights and privileges not accessible to the rest of the saints. This is not the establishing of new promises, but a bringing us back to the same exceeding great and precious promises which are potentially true of everyone who is in Christ. It is not establishing a new foundation, it is calling us back to the Foundation which is already laid.

March 24

"Fulfill my joy by being
like-minded, having the same love,
being of one accord, of one mind."
PHILIPPIANS 2:2

God is working towards a goal: that Christ should have the preeminence in all things. We have observed that this work does not start on the level of "all things," but begins with the individual disciple. From there, God desires a group of people who no longer think and live as mere individuals, only concerned with getting their particular needs met; but are more interested in serving God and meeting the needs of each other. When this occurs (even in a small group of believers) then they can be said to have entered into true spiritual fellowship: one mind and one accord, perfectly adjusted to God and to one another. That does not mean sameness, for every member contributes something unique; but there is a definite unity and a singleness of purpose.

March 25

"The hour is coming, and now is,
when the true worshipers will worship
the Father in spirit and truth; for the Father is
seeking such to worship Him. God is Spirit, and
those who worship Him must worship
in spirit and truth."
JOHN 4:23,24

The corporate Life of God's people will only rise as high as the individuals represented. That is to say, if there is no spirit-and-truth worship in our prayer closet at home, we cannot expect spirit-and-truth worship when we gather together.

So often we come to a gathering expecting to "enter in" to a place in God. Instead, the gathering of believers should be the celebration and continuation of Who we have already entered into.

March 26

"God resists the proud, but gives grace to
the humble. Therefore submit to God. Resist the
devil and he will flee from you."
JAMES 4:6,7

S o many times we try to resist, but we are defeated. Why? Simply because we attempt to resist the devil before we have first submitted ourselves to God. There is a proper order that must be observed without fail.

First, we must understand the principle of God resisting the proud but giving grace to the humble. This is the foundation of everything we do. Second, the word "therefore" signifies that those who learn this principle will act upon it accordingly. If they understand the truth just stated, they will submit "therefore" to God. Third, as a result of their submitting to God, they will find the devil flees whenever and wherever they offer him resistance.

The word "flee" means "to run away in terror." How wonderful! How delicious to see the devil running from us in terror, instead of the other way around!

March 27

"You were slain, and have redeemed
us to God by Your blood out of every tribe
and tongue and people and nation, and have
made us kings and priests to our God;
and we shall reign on the earth."
REVELATION 5:9,10

When we think of a king, we usually think of some human authority exerting their will upon their subjects with a haughty air. But true authority is not found in title or position. Jesus, the King of Kings, shows us that true authority is serving, not lording over. In fact, Psalm 72 tells us what a true king is – someone who serves the people, provides for the poor, and defends those who cannot defend themselves.

We are being prepared for a kingdom. But our preparation is not in learning how to wear a crown or how to walk around with a glorious robe and scepter. One brother sings, "He's brought me low so I could know the way to reach the heights." In God's Kingdom, to go higher, we must go lower. That is the Hidden Wisdom.

March 28

"Narrow is the gate and difficult is
the way which leads to Life."
MATTHEW 7:14

T he Narrow Gate refers to salvation. We know that a gate is an opening, or a door that one passes through. It is an entrance into something. Jesus said, "I am the door. If anyone enters by Me, he will be saved" (John 10:9). Here, Jesus connects the Door, or the Gate, to entering in through Him to be saved. This is the Narrow Gate. Why is it narrow?

The Bible says of Jesus, "Nor is there salvation in any other, for there is no other name under heaven given among men by which we must be saved" (Acts 4:12). To insist that there is no salvation apart from One Man is, in the eyes of the world, rather narrow-minded. But we insist upon it because it is true. Jesus says the Gate is narrow. We must go in through Him. God requires all men to enter in through Christ in order to be saved. There is no way to appropriate the Victory of the Cross without entering in by the One Who was crucified for us.

March 29

"'I am the Alpha and
the Omega, the Beginning and the End,' says
the Lord, 'Who is and Who was and Who
is to come, the Almighty.'"
REVELATION 1:8

J esus is the Alpha from Whom all things in God are initiated, and Jesus is the Omega unto Whom all things of God find their purpose, their meaning, and their reason for being. Everything begins in Christ, and everything ends in Christ. He is the Beginning as well as the End.

Real spiritual growth occurs when we realize that God has only one goal for us, and that is the full, mature, complete, and experiential knowledge of Jesus Christ. To the extent that we discard "things" and become focused wholly on Christ, to that extent we will make progress.

March 30

"If we have been united with Him in a
death like His, we shall certainly be united with
Him in a resurrection like His."
ROMANS 6:5 ESV

I f we share in His death then we will share in
His life. How could it be otherwise? What is
true of the Vine is true of the Branches that are
part of the Vine. It would be impossible for the
Vine to be raised while the Branches that are
part of the Vine remain buried. So long as the
Vine and the Branches are one, they share in
both the suffering and in the glory that is
revealed afterwards.

In the same way, when God made us one
spirit together with Christ on the Cross, His
intention was for us to experience both the
Crucifixion and the Resurrection. So Paul says
that if we suffer with Him, then we will reign
with Him (2 Timothy 2:12). Again, we see the
purpose of the Cross. If we refuse to join Him
in suffering then we cannot hope to join Him in
ruling. If we refuse the Crucified Death then we
cannot have the Resurrected Life.

March 31

"He must increase, but I must decrease."
JOHN 3:30

We must see that everything God has done, everything God is doing, and everything God will do is for the purpose of INCREASING Jesus and DECREASING everything that is not of Him.

This principle is so powerful that it makes no difference if you agree with it, understand it, believe it, or like it. He MUST increase; therefore, He WILL increase and HE IS increasing. At the same time, I MUST decrease, therefore I WILL decrease, and I AM decreasing. This is a spiritual law, and it is working as we speak. For the Christian who is seeking first the Kingdom of God and His Righteousness this is wonderful news. For selfish, carnal Christians it is a frightening thing, this talk of losing your life and taking up your Cross and denying yourself. That is why you hear so much about spiritual power and so little about spiritual brokenness.

April 1

"Jesus took the loaves, and when
He had given thanks He distributed them to
the disciples, and the disciples to those sitting
down; and likewise of the fish, as much as they
wanted. They... filled twelve baskets with the
fragments of the five barley loaves which
were left over by those who had eaten."
JOHN 6:11,13

The issue is never what we have or what we are doing, but rather, do we have the Lord's blessing?

With the Lord's Blessing we have Infinite Supply. Practically speaking, it means instead of trying to convince the Lord to bless what I want to do or what I think needs to be done, I should find out first what the Lord wants to BLESS and do THAT instead. Remember, "He Himself knew what He would do." (John 6:6). Thus, we pray, "Not my will, but Your Will be done; not my kingdom, but Your Kingdom come." And then we enjoy the Lord's Blessing on our work.

April 2

"Blessed are the meek,
for they shall inherit the earth."
MATTHEW 5:5

The idea of the meek inheriting the earth is found throughout the Book of Psalms. When someone is poor in spirit and mourns over his own sins and the sins of others, pride and arrogance are eliminated. A person who knows he is no better than the rest will not be easily lifted up above his brothers and sisters. But this meekness does not imply lack of power, or spineless passivity. It is power, but it is power under the control of love and without the poison of self-interest and self-seeking.

To have power, and to use that power only for the good and well-being of others, is meekness. Jesus perfectly demonstrates how power that operates through meekness cannot be quenched, whereas temporal power and people who play politics always come to a bad end.

April 3

"I in them, and You in Me; that
they may be made perfect in one."
JOHN 17:23

When a symphony performs, each musician has something different to contribute. The title of each piece of music is the same, but there are many different parts that make up that one piece. A musician may be an extremely talented soloist, but playing in harmony with others requires a great deal of practice, preparation and group rehearsal. It also requires each musician to submit to the direction of the conductor. If that means playing "second fiddle" then so be it. Working together takes time and patience – two things that most people do not have an abundance of.

I trust you can see that even in this simple illustration, pride, egotism, and an unwillingness to work with others disqualifies even the greatest musicians from becoming viable members of a symphony. Christ, the Master Conductor, seeks a spiritual harmony among all His disciples: "that they all may be one... that they also may be one in Us" (John 17:21).

April 4

"[Paul and Barnabas] returned...
strengthening the souls of the disciples,
exhorting them to continue in the faith, and
saying, 'We must through many tribulations
enter the kingdom of God.'"
ACTS 14:22

Our idea of overcoming is to avoid tribulation, not pass through it. We certainly do not connect entering the Kingdom with going through tribulation. We think having the victory means eliminating all tribulation. Nothing could be further from the truth.

In order to enter the Kingdom there must be an increase of Christ and a decrease of Self. This is an ongoing process, and by it we judge how far along the Path we have progressed.

But how is Self decreased? The answer is in our circumstances and trials. They are sufficient to decrease us. We need not do anything but wait for them to come, and see them as our opportunity to have Self decreased and Christ increased.

April 5

"If we have been united together in the
likeness of His death, certainly we also shall be in
the likeness of His resurrection."
ROMANS 6:5

It is impossible for us to take up the Cross and not be resurrected. I am almost afraid to make it so plain lest we fail to appreciate its mystery, but it is all there in the Scriptures. We cannot ascend until we have first descended.

Can we embrace the Cross, and love the hands that nail us to it, and hold nothing against the One Who put us there? Can we commit our spirit into His hands and give up Self, looking beyond the present suffering to see the joy that is set before us? This is the way of the Overcomers.

April 6

"No one has ascended to heaven
but He who came down from heaven, that is,
the Son of Man who is in heaven."
JOHN 3:13

No one has ascended because no one can ascend. Rest assured that if it were possible, someone would have done it! But just as we cannot make ourselves acceptable to God on the basis of anything we have done, so too we cannot ascend and seat ourselves at the right hand of God. We are accepted only in the Beloved; we are saved only in the Beloved; and only in the Beloved can we be raised from the dead, ascend and be seated in the heavenlies.

April 7

"He who did not spare His own Son, but
delivered Him up for us all, how shall He not with
Him also freely give us all things?"
ROMANS 8:32

Everyone who looks does not see. Everyone who hears does not listen. What are we looking for? What is it that we need to see? What would God reveal to us? There is but one desire of God for us, and that is that we may see Christ. God does not reveal one hundred, one thousand, or one million things to us. He is pleased to give us His Son, and He delights for us to look only to Him. Not even to the things He gives, but to Him Who is the Gift. We may pray for revelation into a great many matters, but only one thing is important to God, that is, that we may have revelation into the Son.

If we know the Son, if we possess the Son, if we see the Son, we know and possess and see all that God has and is, for He has deposited all of Himself into His Son, and all of His Son He deposited into us.

April 8

"It is the truth concerning
Jesus that inspires all prophecy."
REVELATION 19:10
(Knox)

The prophetic word is given to point us to Jesus. Everything the Holy Spirit would speak, reveal, teach, and show us is towards this same end, which is CHRIST.

We do not need to mull over every dream, vision, word, or prophecy, trying to exegete its hidden meaning, struggling to extract some spiritual significance where none exists. If what we see and hear does not point us to Jesus then it is not prophetic and should be discarded. This simple test will keep us from distraction.

April 9

"He was transfigured before them.
His face shone like the sun, and His clothes
became as white as the light."
MATTHEW 17:2

To be clothed with the Lord Jesus is to be transfigured. For too long we who claim a heavenly calling, a heavenly citizenship, and a heavenly birth have lived as earthly men. What light we have is hidden beneath a bushel; there is no glory that surrounds us. We are not talking about an outward display, or something fleshly, but a Light and a Life which demonstrates the presence of Christ. "In Him was Life – and the Life was the Light of men" (John 1:4).

April 10

"The Law of the Spirit of Life in
Christ Jesus has made me free from
the Law of Sin and Death."
ROMANS 8:2

Two laws are mentioned in this passage of
Scripture: the Law of Life, and the Law of
Sin and Death. We who are in Christ Jesus
have been delivered from the Law of Sin and
Death and are under a new law, which is the
Law of Life. The difference between a
theoretical walk with Christ and a practical
walk with Christ hinges upon being able to
differentiate between the Law of Life and the
Law of Death. In the Garden the choice was
between the Knowledge of Good and Evil (Law
of Death) or the Tree of Life (Law of Life).

We must make the same choice today.
Christians are much exercised in trying to
discern between good and evil, right and
wrong, Spirit and flesh. It seems the more we
try to figure this out the more frustrated we
become. Instead, God would have us come to
the Tree of Life. This Life will instruct us in all
things, including what is right and what is
wrong, yet it is deeper than mere knowledge.

April 11

"Not My will, but Yours, be done."
LUKE 22:42

The Cross demonstrates that we do not gain by trying to get, but by losing in order to gain. We cannot really receive from God until we have learned to give up to God. It is the spirit which cries, "Not my will, but Yours be done" and "Father, into Your Hands I commit my spirit."

These words are easily uttered, but we cannot appreciate them or really experience them until we have been through our Gethsemane experiences and our Golgotha experiences. Until that time we are merely reciting some words, but we do not truly know what it means to give ourselves up to God, to be completely consecrated and submitted to Him. The Cross prepares us to receive by first forcing us to give up. Therefore, the Cross is gaining through losing.

April 12

"That in all things He
may have the preeminence."
COLOSSIANS 1:18

The unavoidable, inevitable conclusion is that Christ will have the preeminence – not just in some things, but in all things. To achieve this, He works one-on-one with His disciples. He then gathers all His disciples together into a spiritual family where they grow and learn together. This spiritual family then invites the rest of the world to join them in giving Christ the preeminence in all things, so that "God may be all in all" (1 Corinthians 15:28).

At the risk of over-simplifying the process, that is the essence of this great movement of God. The point must be reiterated that Jesus is the atoning sacrifice for all sins: "not for ours only but also for the whole world" (1 John 2:2) and He has sent His representatives into "all the world" to "preach the Gospel to every creature" (Mark 16:15).

April 13

"Your kingdom come. Your will
be done on earth as it is in heaven."
MATTHEW 6:10

The chief objective of prayer is to bring us into cooperation with the Father so that we are harmonious with Him – with respect to our love relationship as well as our working relationship. Much time and effort in prayer is spent trying to get God involved with OUR agenda, with OUR plans, with OUR goals, with OUR cause, with OUR needs, real or imagined. But after all, who is the Master? Who is the servant? Whose will are we seeking anyway: ours, or His?

If our agenda is not harmonious with His then our agenda has to go. Most of our prayers are simply too small, too narrow-minded, and too constricted. We do not see anything beyond our present surroundings. We have not seen the big picture. We do not have a heavenly perspective. So to begin with we must empty ourselves of all preconceived ideas and seek the Lord's Will and the Lord's Kingdom when we pray, for this truly honors the Father.

April 14

> "When it pleased God, who separated
> me from my mother's womb and called me
> through His grace, to reveal His Son in me."
> GALATIANS 1:15,16

People sometimes ask me what they have to do to obtain this great revelation of Christ. They think it is God's way of rewarding us for a lot of hard work. Nothing could be further from the truth.

To have one's eyes opened is simply an act of grace, and God alone can do it, and will do it, if we will only ask Him. At the risk of making it sound "too easy," I dare not make it any more difficult than that!

April 15

"Martha, Martha, you are worried and
troubled about many things. But one thing is
needed, and Mary has chosen that good part,
which will not be taken away from her."
LUKE 10:41,42

This One Thing relates to Christ filling all things as the Preeminent One. If we see that God is working all things together according to this Purpose of summing up everything into Christ, towards the One Thing, then we will naturally seek those things which are conducive to this, and we will naturally shun those things which are not.

Later we see Martha continues serving, but everything is all right – there is no complaining about Mary, and everything seems to go on as it should. It is not that service, fellowship, or preparing meals is a bad thing: it simply has to be in the right order. It is not that we cannot perform many good works and spiritual duties, but the work of the Lord must never have preeminence over the Lord of the work.

April 16

"Unless a grain of wheat falls into
the ground and dies, it remains alone; but if it
dies, it produces much grain."
JOHN 12:24

E verything accomplished by way of the Cross brings the fullness of Christ and His Irresistible Kingdom into the heart of every person who believes that He "has blessed us with every spiritual blessing in the heavenly places in Christ" (Ephesians 1:3). This great Gift of Christ has been deposited into the depth of the disciple the same way as a precious seed is buried into the soil. Contained within that seed is a bountiful harvest of rich fruit. But one does not plant a seed on Sunday morning and expect to find fruit on Monday.

The seed must surrender itself to the process of growth before it can mature into something that bears fruit. This amounts to a death, burial, and resurrection.

April 17

"Reckon yourselves to be dead indeed to sin,
but alive to God in Christ Jesus our Lord."
ROMANS 6:11

We do not reckon something to be so after we see it happen, but before we see it happen. What happens if, right after we reckon ourselves dead to sin, we fall back into sin? Does this nullify the Word of God? Does this make God a liar? We can become disappointed and quit (which is what most people do), or we can repent and go right back to reckoning.

Here's what happens: God rewards our reckoning. He delights to see us believing in His Word when it seems impossible! And so He says, "Very well, you have believed having not seen; now you will begin to see the truth of what you have been reckoning!" And eventually we begin to see our reckoning begins to produce fruit. Sin will be broken, not just in theory, but in actual practice. Victory will be ours, not just in principle, but in fact.

April 18

"[God] raised us up together,
and made us sit together in the heavenly
places in Christ Jesus."
EPHESIANS 2:6

Just as certainly as the Vine was crucified, dead, buried, resurrected, ascended and seated, so the Branches were crucified, dead, buried, resurrected, ascended and seated. The whole issue is: will we abide in the Vine and share in the overcoming, or not? Overcoming is bound up with abiding. The Lord says, "Live in Me, and I will live in you."

Now the Lord says that overcomers will sit with Him in His throne. How is that possible? Because we are in Him, and He is in us: "He who is joined to the Lord is one spirit with Him" (1 Corinthians 6:17), and "The two shall become one" (1 Corinthians 6:16).

April 19

"[God] has blessed us
with every spiritual blessing in the
heavenly places in Christ."
EPHESIANS 1:3

All we have and all that we are as Christians is based upon our union with Christ. Apart from Him, we have nothing, and we are nothing. But in Him we are blessed with every spiritual blessing.

Think upon the ramifications of that. If this is true then we have very little to ask God for, and very much to praise God about.

April 20

"Jesus said to him, 'Are you the teacher
of Israel, and do not know these things?'"
JOHN 3:10

W hen you read the Gospels two things
become quite clear. First, Jesus is
undeniably, unquestionably GOD IN THE
FLESH, Wholly Other. Second, the more
religious you are, the less likely it is that you
will see, recognize, and appreciate Him for
Who He really is.

Sinners, on the other hand, had little trouble
recognizing Him. The Samaritan woman may
have been a despised outsider to the Jew's
system of religion, but it only took her a few
minutes to realize that she had found the
Messiah. The Roman centurion, an unworthy
Gentile, nevertheless knew where to go when
his servant was sick, and Jesus said this man's
faith was greater than anyone in Israel. The
Syrophoenician woman had enough faith to ask
Jesus for only a few crumbs from the table, and
even though she was technically not a Jew,
Jesus gave her everything she asked for. Yes,
Jesus was indeed a friend of sinners, publicans,
tax collectors, and women caught in adultery.

April 21

"You were... buried with Him in baptism,
in which you also were raised with Him."
COLOSSIANS 2:12

We can talk about the forces of nature, observe its effects, and sometimes even predict what it will do; but we cannot control it nor do anything about it. Similarly, we can observe the spiritual truths, principles, and laws that make up the Heavenly Order, but we cannot control them or manipulate them to achieve our own ends. In actual experience the invisible seasons of spiritual growth may not be so cut and dry as the visible elements of our world.

Our spiritual journey will probably not correspond with the timely arrangement of the natural seasons. But the periods of life, death, burial, and resurrection in our spiritual walk are as vital to our spiritual growth as the four seasons are necessary to the life of creation. The Heavenly Order exists for our continued spiritual growth and maturity.

April 22

"In Him dwells all the fullness of the Godhead
bodily; and you are complete in Him."
COLOSSIANS 2:9,10

I am afraid that we do not truly appreciate the fact that God has never given us THINGS, but has summed up everything into Christ, having poured Himself into His Son. Having the Son, possessing the Son, being one with the Son, we have and possess everything God is. It never has been a question of seeking ten, one hundred, or one thousand different things from God.

If we do not know from our experience, we should at least know from the Scriptures, that CHRIST IS THE GIFT OF GOD. Then our experience will come into line with God's Thought. If you are used to seeking spiritual "things" (love, joy, peace, anointing, power, blessing, etc.) then this message is particularly for you, but we all stand to benefit from being reminded constantly that Christ is God's One Gift.

April 23

"When Jesus had received the sour wine, He said, 'It is finished!' And bowing His head, He gave up His spirit."
JOHN 19:30

The phrase "it is finished" here is a single word in the Greek: *teleō*. It means, "paid in full," which certainly confirms that Christ has paid the debt of our sins in full. But *teleō* also means the process is completed; the work is fulfilled; in other words, "I have accomplished the purpose for which I came." God is wholly and completely satisfied forever by the one sacrifice of Christ on the Cross. May we never be satisfied with anything less.

Let us lay hold of the complete victory afforded us through Calvary! Let us endeavor to enter into the height, depth, length, width, and breadth of this Cross of Jesus Christ!

April 24

"Always learning, and never able to come
to the knowledge of the truth."
2 TIMOTHY 3:7

I f in our quest for spiritual growth our idea is only to learn a few facts about the Bible, glean tidbits of information from this preacher and that teacher, fill our brains with facts and fill our libraries with more books and magazines, we run the risk of fooling ourselves into thinking that we know and understand God – when it could be that we are ever learning "truths" without knowing the Truth.

Have you met someone like this? They seem to have all the right answers, but they have the wrong spirit. They tenaciously cling to their minute opinions and cannot be persuaded otherwise. Their knowledge has not changed them, except to make them worse: for now they are puffed up in the vanity of their own mind (1 Corinthians 8:1,2). True spiritual growth is characterized by grace (not works) and an increased knowledge of Jesus Christ (2 Peter 3:18). And, we maintain that this knowledge of Jesus Christ cannot be obtained by study, but is only granted by way of revelation.

April 25

"By this My Father is glorified,
that you bear much fruit."
JOHN 15:8

An orange tree is an orange tree as soon as it is planted, even before it produces fruit. It is not an orange tree because it produces oranges; it produces oranges because it is an orange tree. The fruit is the evidence of what it already is. If it were to suddenly produce rotten apples then we know for certain that it is not what we thought it was. The one who has really been saved will produce "much fruit" and will "walk worthy" of their calling (Ephesians 4:1).

That is to say, the evidence of a "born again" person is not in what they say they believe, but in how they actually live. Even the phrase "born again" indicates more than just a change of heart; it represents a spiritual death, burial, and resurrection; a new life. Thus, no one can be truly "born again" until and unless they embrace the Cross, die with Christ, and are raised to Life in Him.

April 26

"He died for all, that those who live
should live no longer for themselves, but for Him
who died for them and rose again."
2 CORINTHIANS 5:15

Not I, but Christ. That is the goal, and the Cross is where the process begins. The crucifixion of Christ is inexorably, inescapably linked to the crucifixion of the disciple. It cannot be otherwise. This is where everything that is Christ's becomes ours as well. On the Cross the two are made one, and the destiny of the One is linked forever with the destiny of the Many.

There in the Cross the Head is joined to the many members of the Body; the Vine is made one with the many branches. "He who is joined to the Lord is one spirit with Him" (1 Corinthians 6:17). Where are they joined? At the Cross. Paul was not there physically when Christ was crucified; yet Paul says, "I am crucified with Christ." Obviously this is a spiritual union, a spiritual oneness.

April 27

"There is no other God
who can deliver like this."
DANIEL 3:29

T he Lord reveals Himself to us when we are
at our end, when the fire burns the hottest.
When we have reached the end of ourselves
then He intervenes. He is committed to us
there in the fire, because we are committed to
Him outside the fire. As we have stood for His
Will and His Kingdom in a state of universal
compromise, darkness, and deception, so He
will stand with us in our state of temptation,
testing, and trial.

Toward what end? That the preeminence we
have been proclaiming may be demonstrated.
He will rise to the occasion and prove Himself
faithful.

April 28

"As many of you as were baptized
into Christ have put on Christ."
GALATIANS 3:27

What does it mean to be baptized? It is to go down into death and to come back up into Life. We were baptized into Christ. The water of baptism does not merely signify the washing away of sins, but the death of the sinner. We go down into the water, and we are brought up out of the water. If we were to stay under the water for long we would surely die. But we are quickly lifted back up out of the "grave." This represents death and resurrection.

The outward sign of water baptism is meant to represent an inward spiritual truth – that I am baptized indeed, not into water only, but into Christ. I died with Him, and I was raised with Him. If I am one with Him then His death is my death; when He is raised, I too am raised. God has placed us in Christ, and since we are joined to the Lord, we are one spirit with Him. The Branches will go the way of the Vine. The Body will go the way of the Head.

April 29

"In Him dwells all the fullness of the
Godhead bodily; and you are complete in Him,
who is the head of all principality and power."
COLOSSIANS 2:9,10

Everything God has done, is doing, and will
do is aimed at bringing us deeper into
Christ, to finish what was begun in us when we
first received Him. God is the One Who brings
us through the Gate, and God is the One Who
leads us along the Path.

Everything God has done, is doing, and will
do has the same purpose, and that purpose
explains everything you have been through,
everything you are going through, and
everything you will go through.

April 30

"All things were created
through Him and for Him."
COLOSSIANS 1:16

I n the beginning, when man walked with God, there was an obvious Heavenly Order in the earth. This simply meant that Christ was in His rightful place. When Christ has the preeminence, when He has the centrality and the supremacy, then all is well.

God created all things "by Him and for Him" and installed Him as Lord of All. With Christ in His rightful place the rest of creation could proceed. Six times in the Book of Genesis God declared that what He had just made was "good." When the work was finally completed, God judged the final state of things to be "very good" (Genesis 1:31) and by far the greatest benefit of living under this Heavenly Order was the spiritual condition of man before the fall. Spiritually he was at peace with himself and at peace with his God. In a word, the state of things as they existed in the Heavenly Order was perfect. It was, quite literally, heaven on earth.

May 1

"One thing I know: that though
I was blind, now I see."
JOHN 9:25

We are the man born blind in John 9. It is not that he can improve himself, or gradually come to the place where he can see something. He is BORN blind, and he can see nothing but darkness until the Lord, the Light of the world, makes him see.

So many blind people hope to improve their seeing through sermons, meetings, and more teachings. But one moment of seeing is worth ten thousand years of learning. It is better to sit at the feet of an ignorant man who has seen the Lord than it is to be instructed by the most educated Bible teacher who is blind to the things of God.

May 2

"Narrow is the gate and
difficult is the way which leads to life,
and there are few who find it."
MATTHEW 7:14

We cannot walk the narrow path until we have entered the narrow gate. But we cannot assume that because we have entered the narrow gate we are now finished. Most people lay stress on the gate, and their goal is to get people just far enough through the gate that they can claim salvation. But the narrow gate is only the beginning.

The narrow gate only opens the door to the narrow way. It is the *narrow way* which leads to Life, and few find it. Fewer still walk to the end of it.

May 3

"When they had gone through
Phrygia and the region of Galatia, they
were forbidden by the Holy Spirit to preach the
word in Asia. After they had come to Mysia,
they tried to go into Bithynia, but the Spirit
did not permit them."
ACTS 16:6,7

Our destination, as well as our departure, must be governed by the Spirit. How intriguing that the Spirit actually forbade them to preach the word in Asia and Bithynia! This ought to be proof enough that "need," in and of itself, is insufficient guidance. The only thing that matters is being sent, and it is critical that we go only where the Spirit sends us.

The apostles were indeed sent forth by the Spirit, yet that same Spirit did not permit them to just go wherever they pleased. Later we see that Paul indeed went to Asia and a tremendous work was founded. This tells us that a "no" today does not mean a "no" is forever; nevertheless, when the Spirit forbids us, we dare not take matters into our own hands and go where we have not been sent.

May 4

"I know that in me (that is,
in my flesh) nothing good dwells."
ROMANS 7:18

Paul knew this because he knew the Cross. Do we know it? Those who embrace the Cross have acknowledged this in themselves and have surrendered their way over to His Way.

In what areas must we acknowledge this inability to do anything apart from Christ? It must not only be acknowledged: it must be truly seen, deeply felt, and painfully experienced in every area of our life, one step at a time. This is the work of the Cross. In our daily life we come up against situations that we cannot overcome in our own strength, or with our own wisdom. We need a strength and a wisdom that comes from Above, that comes from Beyond, that comes from Another outside of us and yet rises up from within us.

May 5

"He raised Him from the dead and seated
Him at His right hand in the heavenly places, far
above all principality and power."
EPHESIANS 1:20,21

You will find that the whole strategy of the adversary is to bring you down from your heavenly position in Christ and engage you on a fleshly, carnal, earthly level. To overcome, you need only maintain the ascended position with Christ. We are not trying to get the victory. Instead, we have been made one *with* Victory. If I enter into a room and sit down in a chair I do not have to wonder how I will enter the room. God has already seated us together with Christ; therefore, we do not have to try to enter in, rise up, or "get" the victory. Having already obtained this triumph through the Cross, we no longer have to attain it in our own strength. The Cross of Christ! What a marvelous provision it is!

May 6

"We know that when He is
revealed, we shall be like Him, for
we shall see Him as He is."
1 JOHN 3:2

I f we are abiding in Him then we will be as
He is. If we have put on the Lord Jesus then
we are being changed into His likeness, we are
being made into His image, and we are in the
process of being transfigured.

After some time following the Lord we
should not have to stop and ask ourselves,
"What would Jesus do?" If we are being
transfigured then that Light and that Life will
respond spontaneously and effortlessly to any
demand placed upon it.

May 7

"Rejoice in Christ Jesus, and
have no confidence in the flesh."
PHILIPPIANS 3:3

S elf – meaning the innate tendency in man to put himself and his desires above God and others – is the real source of all wickedness. That explains why merely dealing with the devil is not enough to rid the world of evil. If the devil were to disappear tomorrow the problem of Self would remain. It is a condition that exists deep within every man, woman, boy, and girl. Although the Self-life is a formidable obstacle to the Christ-life, it is by no means too difficult for God to overcome. Christ must increase, and Self must decrease. God is working to reestablish and recover that Heavenly Order in all things, beginning with individuals, then with a company of men and women, and ultimately extending to the entire creation, so that "God may be all in all" (1 Corinthians 15:28). The Bible is the story of the progressive recovery and increase of Christ in the midst of a world gone astray.

May 8

"I take pleasure in infirmities, in
reproaches, in needs, in persecutions, in
distresses, for Christ's sake. For when I am
weak, then I am strong."
2 CORINTHIANS 12:10

Now it does not say that Paul made himself weak on purpose. We do not have to seek weaknesses, infirmities, tribulations, temptations, or trials. We already have them. The key is how do we respond to them? We can fight them, or we can embrace them. Paul clearly shows us that it is not always God's will for us to be saved FROM the fire. Often we are called to walk THROUGH the fire, with no assurance except that His Grace is sufficient. In the fire we learn that "Grace" is a Man, just like Victory is a Man.

To be delivered from weakness is one thing, but to meet Grace in my weakness is something else entirely.

May 9

"Noah found grace in the eyes of the Lord."
GENESIS 6:8

It took five hundred years of walking with God, but Noah found grace, and that made it all worthwhile. Let us learn to do nothing apart from this amazing grace. It is better to wait five hundred years for grace than to work for five minutes without it.

What is grace? I teach people that Grace is a Man. Amazing Grace is simply Jesus living in me, doing what I cannot do. It does not matter if "what I cannot do" is save myself, overcome sin, love my neighbor, or build an ark. "For by Grace (Jesus) you have been saved through faith (trusting Jesus to do what you cannot do); and that not of yourselves; it (He) is the Gift of God" (Ephesians 2:8). I am insufficient; but His Grace (Jesus) is sufficient. His Grace (Jesus) is more than enough. His Grace (Jesus) is Infinite Supply! But "without Me you can do nothing" (John 15:5).

May 10

"May [God] give to you the spirit of wisdom
and revelation in the knowledge of Him."
EPHESIANS 1:17

T he Lord reveals Himself to us in a variety
of ways, and every testimony is different.
Peter received the revelation of Christ while
fishing. But Thomas received the revelation of
Christ only after the Lord appeared to Him and
showed him His wounds. Paul received the
revelation of Christ on the road to Damascus,
as he was on his way to kill Christians. One
man says Christ was revealed to him as he
stood watching a tree in the dead of winter.
Christ was revealed to me as I sat in my
backyard, arguing with the Lord over the Bible.

What do these experiences have in common?
They are spontaneous unveilings of Jesus
Christ. Without warning the Lord simply
reveals Himself, and whereas we were blind
before, today we see. It is like walking out of
one room and into another room, closing the
door behind us.

May 11

"If anyone desires to come
after Me, let him deny himself, and take up
his cross daily, and follow Me."
LUKE 9:23

D o we need the power of God today? Do we seek the Life of the Lord today? Do we desire Him to have the preeminence in our lives today? Do we long for Him today? Then now is the time for us to be unconditionally and wholeheartedly surrendered to Him. We need not drag the process out for several days and weeks, months and years. Do it today, do it now.

If we must daily take up the Cross anyway, let us bow our head and give up the ghost instead of struggling to stay alive, which only prolongs our agony. The secret to overcoming is dying daily.

May 12

"I have been crucified with Christ; it is no
longer I who live, but Christ lives in me."
GALATIANS 2:20

Just as salvation is ours through faith by grace, and not of ourselves, so it is with living the Christian life. The difference between a defeated Christian and a victorious Christian is simply this: the former lives by his own power and asks for God's help and will almost as an afterthought, while the latter despairs of himself, lays down his life, and trusts Christ to live in his place, at all times.

The Cross is how God accomplishes this task of bringing us to the end of ourselves. Then we can say, "Not I, but Christ."

May 13

"Thanks be to God, who gives us the
victory through our Lord Jesus Christ."
1 CORINTHIANS 15:57

When God is pleased to reveal His Son to us, we will learn that Victory is not a thing, but a Person; that Victory is not an experience, but a Man; that God does not give me a thing called victory, but has given me His Son in the place of victory in order to be my Victory. Then Victory will never be future-tense and far-away, but Ever Present and Now. For Victory is Christ. And Victory lives within you.

Thus, Victory has nothing to do with the devil, and everything to do with Christ. Since most Christians have more faith, assurance and reverence for the devil than they do for the Lord Jesus, it is easy to see why so many are defeated.

May 14

"I have come that they may have life, and
that they may have it more abundantly."
JOHN 10:10

Ask the Lord to open your eyes and show
you the Life which is yours. Go to Him and
say, "I have heard about this Life, but I don't
know how it works or what to do with it. Please
show me, please teach me, please reveal this
Life to me." And He will do it.

If ever you see this, just once, you will
discover the secret to the Christian life. You
will shake your head and say, "All these years I
thought I was really living the Christian life,
and all I have been doing is playing
tiddlywinks. This Life I have been given is
greater, bigger, and more wonderful than I ever
dreamed!"

May 15

"Elisha prayed, and said, 'Lord, I pray,
open his eyes that he may see.' Then the LORD
opened the eyes of the young man, and he saw.
And behold, the mountain was full of horses
and chariots of fire all around Elisha."
2 KINGS 6:17

D enying the existence of the adversary will not make him disappear. We acknowledge and admit that there is a real enemy, a real spirit of Antichrist, that is out to destroy the Remnant and hinder the Testimony of Jesus. We also acknowledge and admit that more often than not, this spirit of Antichrist seems to get the advantage over us.

Even so, the issue is not the enemy. We may look at the enemy, study him, and build an entire movement around different ways to fight him. We can write books and hold seminars on "spiritual warfare." But when we look out from the mountain, what do we really see? Here is the difference between those who overcome and those who are defeated: it is not in their ability to fight, but in their ability to SEE, and this seeing is not of themselves, but is of God.

May 16

"Seek the kingdom of God, and all
these things shall be added to you."
LUKE 12:31

Let us seek first the Kingdom of God – not as an idea, or a doctrine, or a theological position, but as a way of living! At least Paul could say, "my speech and my preaching were not with persuasive words of human wisdom, but in demonstration of the Spirit and of power" (1 Corinthians 2:4). Is anyone frustrated by the fact that all too often the only thing we have to offer people in the name of Jesus are pretty words?

At some point sermons and songs fail and something of the very Life and power and glory and majesty of God must come forth to meet real, practical needs. Healing the sick and casting out devils was (and is) as much a part of the Kingdom of God as preaching and teaching. Everyone we pray for is not instantly healed and delivered, but let us pray for them anyway. We may not yet see all things submitted to Him, but can we not at least expect to see some things submitted to Him?

May 17

"I am the bread of life. He who comes
to Me shall never hunger, and he who believes
in Me shall never thirst."
JOHN 6:35

The Law of Life says that the presence of Christ within the believer results in spiritual satisfaction. If we have Him then we will never hunger or thirst again, because He is Infinite Supply.

Anything less than spiritual satisfaction indicates that there is a problem. I am not saying that one should be content with their progress and present knowledge of Christ so that they stop growing; but I am saying that no matter what stage of progress you may be at presently, Christ should be your satisfaction.

May 18

"I know that in me (that is, in
my flesh) nothing good dwells."
ROMANS 7:18

It is a great day for the Lord when a disciple of Jesus learns this most basic lesson: that in "me," in myself, in my flesh, dwells no good thing.

This is a very difficult thing for people to learn. Jesus says that without Him we can do nothing (John 15:5). This verse is very well-known. Even so, Christians still attempt to do many things apart from the Lord. We feel like we simply must do something, anything. And even though the Bible says there is nothing good in our flesh, and the flesh profits nothing, we spend a lot of time doing fleshly things apart from the Spirit of Jesus, thinking they are good and profitable.

It is impossible to say for sure just how many of the things we "feel led" to do and say are actually just things *we* feel like doing and saying. A lot of the time the Lord has very little to do with it.

May 19

"All we like sheep have gone astray; we
have turned every one, to his own way."
ISAIAH 53:6

Sheep are notorious for going their own
independent way and ignoring the
Shepherd. The Shepherd is well able to protect
His Sheep; the Shepherd's challenge is to get
the Sheep to stay close to Him at all times. To
accomplish this He has to discipline us severely
and teach us not to wander off. This is where
the work of the Cross comes in.

But what a great day for both the Shepherd
and the stubborn little sheep when it no longer
goes its own way, but follows the Shepherd and
obeys His voice! Were it not for Him the lambs
would be destroyed in a moment.

May 20

"He who has the Son has life; he who does not
have the Son of God does not have life."
1 JOHN 5:12

Would it shock you to learn that God has not given us a thing called eternal life? The Apostle John made this quite clear in his inspired writings, saying first of all, in the oft-quoted John 3:16, that the Son is that which was given, and eternal life is simply the reward for those who receive the Son.

It becomes even more apparent in 1 John 5:12. Yes we are given Eternal Life, true, but the Life is not floating out in space somewhere waiting to fall on those who ask. Eternal Life has nothing to do with everlasting existence. Eternal Life is a Person; the Life is the Son; hence, we need only ask if we have received Jesus and we shall know whether we have Eternal Life. The Life is bound up in the Son, as is every one of God's precious gifts. Having the Son, we therefore have all the Son has. Eternal Life is simply an alias for Christ.

May 21

"Whoever desires to save his life
will lose it, but whoever loses his life for
My sake will find it."
MATTHEW 16:25

Some will say, "I am willing to die now that I have followed." The person who knows the Cross says, "I am fit to follow now that I have died."

Why is this important? Because Jesus knows that no human being is qualified to follow Him until they have first died. Jesus knows a man cannot live until he has died and been raised to life again. He therefore bids us to die right away, that He may raise us from the dead by His Indwelling Spirit and place us immediately upon the correct path.

May 22

"Arise therefore, go down and go with them,
doubting nothing; for I have sent them."
ACTS 10:20

The success of the mission to Cornelius' house had less to do with Peter's ability to speak and more to do with the audience's ability to hear. When we speak only to whom we are sent then we will see dramatic results.

Trying to speak to everyone in general and no one in particular is a colossal waste of time and demonstrates poor stewardship. We ought not to give ten coins to someone who can only handle five, and we ought not to give five coins to someone who cannot handle even one. It is clear that much time is wasted trying to convince, persuade, plead, argue, teach, and help people to whom God has not sent us. If we will wait for the Spirit of God we will save ourselves a lot of time, effort and energy. A worker who indiscriminately throws precious seed on rocky ground and gives pearls to pigs is not being a wise, faithful, and profitable servant.

May 23

"Whoever does not bear his cross and
come after Me cannot be My disciple."
LUKE 14:27

E mbracing the Cross is not a once-and-for-
all act, but a daily attitude of knowing our
insufficiency in order to know the sufficiency of
Christ. Jesus asks us to take up the Cross
"daily" (Luke 9:23) and Paul said "I die daily"
(1 Corinthians 15:31). Since we daily meet with
temptations, tests and trials, so we must daily
affirm and reaffirm who we are in Christ: the
crucified, dead, buried, resurrected, ascended
and seated Branches of the crucified, dead,
buried, resurrected, ascended, and seated Vine.

As disciples we take up the Cross daily,
which means we are always in a state of
surrender and submission to the Lord Jesus,
constantly forsaking our own way for His Way.
This moment-by-moment yielding to Him is
summed up in this saying: "Not I, but Christ"
(Galatians 2:20).

May 24

"I have been crucified with Christ; it is
no longer I who live, but Christ lives in me."
GALATIANS 2:20

This is the beginning point of our identification: crucifixion with Christ. Here Paul tells us the secret of what it means to be a disciple. A Christian is not someone who believes certain things about Jesus and tries to live a good life. A Christian is someone who is crucified with Christ and has no life of his own.

"Not I, but Christ" is not just the secret of living the Christian life, it is the goal and the end result of all God's dealings with us along the lines of discipleship. He must increase. I must decrease. Follow this process out to its inevitable, irresistible conclusion and you see that eventually there is none of me; it is all of Him in me.

May 25

"God also bearing witness both with signs
and wonders, with various miracles, and gifts of
the Holy Spirit, according to His own will."
HEBREWS 2:4

When people are healed and delivered it gives us a taste of what conditions are like when Christ has preeminence over all things. Miracles give us a glimpse of a future time when He will make all things new and there will be "no more death, nor sorrow, nor crying. There shall be no more pain, for the former things have passed away" (Revelation 21:4). What we consider miraculous in this Age will be commonplace in the Age to come.

May 26

"They overcame [the dragon] by the
blood of the Lamb, and by the word of their
testimony; and they did not love
their lives to the death."
REVELATION 12:11

Just as there is no victory without a fight, no Crown without a Cross, so there is no Testimony without a devil. Our Testimony is not a thing that is said, but it is a LIFE that is lived. We overcome the Dragon by the word of this Testimony. This Testimony demonstrates the preeminence of Christ over sin, self, and satan: and it is a violent thing, a proactive thing, not a passive thing. The Lord's Testimony is actually strengthened when the enemy comes against it, for in the end we see that Christ is, indeed, preeminent. If we are really demonstrating this then we should be getting stronger spiritually.

That is not to say we will always feel good and always have a smile on our face while engaging the enemy. But regardless of our outward condition, our inward condition will be continually strengthened as we bear the Testimony of Jesus.

May 27

"God, who is rich in mercy, because
of His great love with which He loved us... raised
us up together, and made us sit together in the
heavenly places in Christ Jesus."
EPHESIANS 2:4,6

The difference between those who overcome and those who do not overcome is a difference in their own PERCEIVED position. We all ought to perceive that in Christ we are seated in the heavenly places. We cannot overcome without this perception, this seeing, this revelation. If our perception is earthly, we will remain earthly. If our perception is heavenly, we will overcome.

May 28

"Blessed are you, Simon Bar-Jonah, for
flesh and blood has not revealed this to you, but
My Father who is in heaven."
MATTHEW 16:17

Here, Jesus contrasts "flesh and blood" knowledge with Truth which is revealed by God (and of course, Jesus is Truth [John 14:6]). The two are as different as night and day. In the matter of flesh and blood knowledge that is obtained from human, earthly sources, we may have reason to boast in our ability to study, investigate, reason, and decide. This is the Tree of Knowledge.

In the case of revelation, we have definitely no room to boast, for revelation is simply that which is revealed to us from heaven by the Lord. We cannot work to obtain it nor do we merit it. Additionally, no man may give it to us. Its source is God working in us through His Holy Spirit. This is the Tree of Life.

May 29

"I have suffered the loss of all things…
that I may know Him and the power of His
resurrection, and the fellowship of His sufferings,
being conformed to His death."
PHILIPPIANS 3:8,10

A disciple of Jesus is not someone who mentally embraces the idea of a crucified Christ, nor is it someone who simply reads and accepts the historical record of the crucifixion. A disciple of Jesus is one who enters into the *experience* of the Cross and is personally acquainted and familiar with it. He has taken up his own Cross and followed in the footsteps of Christ. The objective work of the Cross was accomplished when Christ was crucified; the subjective work of the Cross is accomplished when I daily deny myself, take up my Cross, and follow after Him. His work on the Cross is finished and complete; my work through the Cross is ongoing. The Cross He bore accomplished the work of redemption, while the Cross I bear accomplishes the work of spiritual maturity.

May 30

"When I am weak, then I am strong."
2 CORINTHIANS 12:10

T he way of the world says that in order to be stronger, we must build ourselves up and seek strength and dominance over others. Christians everywhere are keenly interested in how to be increased, how to be stronger, how to take authority, how to rise up, how to get more. They look for methods, formulas, and techniques for becoming bigger and better. The results have been disappointing. Many mistakes have been made and many people have been hurt and disillusioned.

The Lord has a different approach for us to take. He invites us to accept weakness in order to be strengthened. We do not become strong by embracing strength, but by embracing weakness! This is the secret of all spiritual power. When Paul learned this secret he was able to say, "When I am weak, then I am strong." This makes no sense to the natural man.

May 31

"We regard no one according to the flesh.
Even though we have known Christ according to
the flesh, yet now we know Him thus no longer."
2 CORINTHIANS 5:16

In our relationships it is easy to touch one another in the flesh. But to put on the Lord Jesus is to make no provision for the flesh, even in our relationships. To "know no man after the flesh" is truly a challenge. We "project" a certain something, and either it is ourselves, or it is Christ.

We note the personality differences between Paul, and Peter, and John, and James, and Barnabas; even so, they each have the same clothing, having put on the Lord Jesus. So we can touch them on a deeper level than who they are in themselves. We can still see the man, but we mostly see the Lord of the man. When we put on the Lord Jesus then the outward man becomes consistent with the inward man. This is fruitfulness, and this should be the normal experience of all disciples of the Lord.

June 1

"Be renewed in the spirit of your mind."
EPHESIANS 4:23

When we embrace the Cross in our thought life we will see that our own thinking is limited, and at times, completely the opposite of God's thoughts. We will readily see that our opinions, our prejudices, our very point of view, all need radical transformation. We will see how untrustworthy and unpredictable our mind, will and emotions can be apart from God.

As we submit ourselves to the Cross we see that God does not turn us into unthinking, unfeeling creatures of wood or stone; instead, He renews and transforms our mind so that our thoughts reflect His thoughts, and our mind reflects His mind. We will no longer be carried away by our emotions or find false comfort in our superior intellect. Our thoughts will be submitted to His wisdom and will assist us in understanding His Will and His Ways.

June 2

"You have come to Mount Zion
and to the city of the living God,
the heavenly Jerusalem."
HEBREWS 12:22

All the prophets pointed to Jerusalem as the place where the Messiah would rule and reign. On the surface this seems self-evident. The trouble with this is that the nature of the Kingdom is spiritual, and so the location of the Kingdom is likewise spiritual. A spiritual kingdom is not going to have an earthly capital. Neither will it have an earthly temple, an earthly priesthood, or an earthly King. It will be in the earth, but it will not rise up from the earth.

Earthly problems cannot be solved with earthly solutions. Earthly problems require Heavenly solutions. The fact that John saw the New Jerusalem coming down out of Heaven and settling upon the earth shows that this is something established by God Himself, quite beyond the command and control of man.

June 3

"As you received Christ Jesus
the Lord [the Narrow Gate], so walk in
Him [the Narrow Path]."
COLOSSIANS 2:6 ESV

We come to the Lord admitting that we cannot save ourselves, and He does the saving. That is the Gate. Now we come to the Lord every day, admitting that we cannot enter the Kingdom, and He does what it takes to conform us into His image. That is the Path.

Hence, I have no secret for the Christian Life, but Christ. I have no key, but Christ. I have no method, but Christ. I have no formula, but Christ. I have no technique, but Christ. I have no life, but Christ – for it is no longer I who lives, it is Christ Who lives in me (Galatians 2:20). In Him, through Him, because of Him, and by Him we may enter the Kingdom.

June 4

"Simon answered and said to Him,
'Master, we have toiled all night and caught
nothing; nevertheless at Your word I will let down
the net.' And when they had done this, they
caught a great number of fish,
and their net was breaking."
LUKE 5:5,6

To you and me this may sound like a coincidence, or luck. Some might call it a miracle, and it is miraculous, but it is more than a miracle; it is a sign given by Christ in order to reveal Himself to Peter. In Scriptural language, it is "revealing His glory."

Jesus merely said, "Launch out into the deep and let down your nets for a catch of fish." Nevertheless, Peter perceived that Jesus was no ordinary man. For when he saw what happened, he fell down and sobbed, "Lord, depart from me, for I am a sinful man." The One he called Teacher he now calls Lord, and Peter is immediately made to see the contrast of himself, a sinful man, and Christ, the Holy One of God. Everyone else heard the teaching, but Peter saw the Person.

June 5

"Blessed are those who hunger and thirst
for righteousness, for they will be filled."
MATTHEW 5:6

To hunger and thirst for righteousness is to look forward to the promise of new heavens and a new earth (2 Peter 3:13): to long for it, to desire it, to pine for it, to seek it, to prepare for it and to keep praying for it until it arrives. It implies that we are not content with things just the way they are, and we are not satisfied to just let things go along as they always have.

We hate sin, we hate the effects of sin upon this earth, and we mourn the consequences of man's inhumanity to man and rebellion towards God; but we have hope for a better day, a better life, a better world where Righteousness Himself is living among us. Until such time, we are hungry and thirsty for more of what we have only just begun to taste.

June 6

"Most gladly I will rather boast in my infirmities,
that the power of Christ may rest upon me."
2 CORINTHIANS 12:9

All those who want power with God must see that His power is released through our weakness. Do realize that you are weak whether you admit it or not, but the power of humility is in recognizing and agreeing before God that we really can do nothing of our own selves.

God's power is not for those with natural charisma, talent, leadership skills, education, training, or "connections." God is not looking for volunteers to serve at their own convenience as their schedule permits, but calls for disciples who will lay down their lives. The flesh counts for nothing in spiritual matters.

June 7

"We who live are always delivered
to death for Jesus' sake."
2 CORINTHIANS 4:11

T he answer to why there is so little power and genuine spiritual fruit in the lives of those who follow Jesus is a simple one: they desire the Life of the Lord, but not His Death. They want a daily pouring out of the Lord's Life, but they shun the prospect of daily sharing in His Death.

The saints of the Lord are well instructed in living victoriously, being blessed, walking in power, overcoming the enemy, and living up to their potential. By comparison, the majority of them know next to nothing about self-denial, bearing their Cross, boasting in their weaknesses, being joyful in trials, winning by losing, gaining by giving up, working by resting, accepting both the bitter and the sweet as gifts from God, enduring hardness and accepting suffering. God desires to increase us and enlarge us; He therefore calls us to go back to the Cross and start over again.

June 8

"You know Him; for He dwells
with you, and will be in you."
JOHN 14:17

J ust as Testimony follows Revelation, so Life
follows Light. We simply know what to do
because He Himself is doing it through us. If
we have put on the Lord Jesus then we need
not look to the past, or to the future. We need
not look up to the heavens, or down upon the
earth. We need not look outward at all, for the
Kingdom of God is within us.

The One Who said, "I am with you, and will
be in you" has now taken up residence within
all who believe.

June 9

"The Truth shall make you free."
JOHN 8:32

The Cross must be embraced and taken up daily as a principle of living. This is the practical application of taking up the Cross. If we ever lay down the Cross and attempt anything in our own power then we will be defeated. But as we continually reckon ourselves "dead indeed to sin but alive to God in Christ" (Romans 6:11) then what is true in principle eventually becomes true in our experience: sin begins to lose its power to control us, and we begin to see that we do have a choice.

We will begin to see that we are no longer slaves to sin, but "if the Son makes you free, you shall be free indeed" (John 8:36).

June 10

"He is able even to subdue
all things to Himself."
PHILIPPIANS 3:21

W hat a mighty God we serve! Exactly how the Lord goes about bringing all things into submission unto Himself is... how can we describe it? It is an art. It is a science. There is a process at work in this universe. Do you see it? It is a process through which the Lord is continually refining, purging, molding, chastening, disciplining, judging, and conforming all things. This process is working itself out on every level, from galaxies, to nations, to the innermost recesses of the souls of men, right down to the very last disciple and sinner.

Throw yourself onto the Rock and be broken; or wait for it to fall on you and be ground into powder (Luke 20:18, Daniel 2:34,35). Either way, sooner or later, the Rock wins, for "He MUST increase, but I MUST decrease" (John 3:30).

June 11

"Love your enemies, bless those who curse you, do good to those who hate you, and pray for those who spitefully use you and persecute you."
MATTHEW 5:44

The nature of the Kingdom of God is quite different, and its character reflects that difference. There is not a kingdom on the face of the earth that could ever adopt a philosophy that says "love your enemies." If you accept the premise that Jesus really is a King then you are compelled to acknowledge that this King and His Kingdom are truly not of this world.

A national defense policy based on "Love Your Enemies" would be political and national suicide for any earthly government. This Heavenly Order is such a radical departure from the ways of the world that it requires some rather deep experiences with God before a person can really enter into the service of the King, because that service is so unlike anything anyone has ever seen or experienced.

June 12

"In [Christ] are hidden all the treasures
of wisdom and knowledge."
COLOSSIANS 2:3

I t is not that God gives us revelation into five, ten, one hundred, or one thousand things. None of these "things" by themselves really matter. Rather, He has placed all those "things" within Christ, and reveals Christ to us. He will not reveal anything to us apart from the Revelation of Jesus Christ. To possess the Son is to possess all that pertains to the Son, for the Scriptures declare, "He who did not spare His own Son, but delivered Him up for us all, how shall He not with Him also freely give us all things?" (Romans 8:32). It is not that God desires to give us revelation into these many things, but for us to have the Revelation of Jesus Christ. By apprehending Him we will subsequently gain insight in those "things." To seek revelation into the "things" apart from the Revelation of Christ fails to give Christ the preeminence. We dare not circumvent the knowledge of Him in the pursuit of "things," even spiritual things, for they are all summed up into Him.

June 13

"Humble yourselves under the mighty hand
of God, that He may exalt you in due time."
1 PETER 5:6

When we are submitted to the Lord, we find Grace. We find Peace. We find Rest. All things are in His hands, and He does all things well. We need not fear what any devil or any man can do to us. To be submitted to the Lord is to be under His care, under His guidance, under His power, under His protection. Whom shall I fear? What can man do to me? What can the devil do to me?

If I have humbled myself beneath the mighty hand of God then He will exalt me in due season; He will justify me; He will defend me; He will fight for me. If our submission to God is complete, if our surrender to the Lord is total, then victory is assured.

June 14

"Peter said to Jesus, 'Master, it is good for us
to be here; and let us make three tabernacles.'"
LUKE 9:33

Christians seek many spiritual things: anointing, power, gifts, blessing, fruit, wisdom, prosperity. I pray the Lord will make us thoroughly and completely dissatisfied with THINGS, even the things He gives us, and make us hungry and thirsty for Himself.

May we judge things not by whether they are "good for us," but whether they are good for the Lord, whether His Will is done in them, whether His Need is met by them, whether His Purpose is fulfilled in them, whether His Son is seen through them. He is the Only One, the Beloved Son of God. May the Lord be transfigured before us!

June 15

"He who overcomes, I will make
him a pillar in the temple of My God,
and he shall go out no more."
REVELATION 3:12

Overcomers are pillars in the temple of God. It is not a question of how many times can we "attend" something, but whether or not we are abiding at all times. Pillars are an integral part of the structure; if they were to suddenly "go out," the building would collapse.

What are we saying? That God's highest is not for us to come in and to go out, but to be a pillar. Overcomers are pillars in the temple of God, and that is a heavenly matter. However you wish to interpret this, one thing is clear: they have learned how to minister to the Lord continually, regardless of time or place. It is Spirit and Truth worship the Father seeks, and they give Him what He is looking for. There is no holy day or sacred hour or special devotion. They do not have to "come into" the presence of the Lord because they LIVE IN the presence of the Lord continually. And so they overcome the earthly by abiding in the heavenly.

June 16

"I am the bread of life. He who comes
to Me shall never hunger, and he who
believes in Me shall never thirst."
JOHN 6:35

S o how do we touch Him directly? "He who
comes to Me." Can it really be this easy? A
better question is: why should it be difficult? I
can come to Him whether I am driving down
the street, walking down the sidewalk, or
sitting in my chair. I can come to Him whether
it is Sunday morning or Tuesday night or
Friday afternoon. I can come to Him in a large
group, or with two or three, or all by myself. I
can come to Him in the desert, in the garden,
in the church building, or in the prison camp. I
am prevented from doing many things due to
circumstance, location, state of mind, or
resources. But one thing I cannot be prevented
from doing is coming to the Lord.

June 17

"When Daniel knew that the writing
was signed, he went home. And in his upper
room, with his windows open toward Jerusalem,
he knelt down on his knees three times that day,
and prayed and gave thanks before his God, as
was his custom since early days."
DANIEL 6:10

I have found through personal experience that the lion's den usually comes about the same time as the revelation. The burden to pray comes with the edict forbidding prayer; Daniel labors for God's purpose while Daniel's enemies labor for his death; the answer comes along with a death sentence. This is not unusual, but quite common. Apostolic revelation and apostolic persecution go hand-in-hand. Revelation does not come to us apart from our circumstance, our environment, our struggle, our wrestling. Many want the revelation but they do not want the lion's den. They want the angels but not the enemies. Yet the depth of the revelation is measured by the depth of the suffering, and if our sufferings are light, then our revelation is shallow.

June 18

"I say, through the grace given to me,
to everyone who is among you, not to think of
himself more highly than he ought to think."
ROMANS 12:3

We do not need Self-Esteem, we need Christ-Esteem. The more we see of Jesus the less we will trust in ourselves.

That is why, once Paul learned his lesson, he wrote, "We have no confidence in the flesh" (Philippians 3:3). He then goes on to list quite a number of things that seem important in terms of religion, status, social order, education, and good works – all the things that tend to make one self-confident and self-righteous. With one grand stroke, Paul says, "Yet, I count them all as dung, that I may win Christ." He simply discards what some people spend a lifetime trying to achieve. Here is a man who knows the sufficiency of God as well as the insufficiency of himself.

June 19

"They overcame [the dragon] by the
blood of the Lamb, and by the word of their
testimony; and they did not love
their lives to the death."
REVELATION 12:11

No one can overcome a spiritual adversary unless they embrace the Cross. The ones who overcome the dragon do so by the blood of the Lamb and by not loving their own lives. Their testimony is: "not I, but Christ." The blood, and loving not their life, and their testimony, all point to the same thing: these are people of the Cross. They did not love their own lives, but they gave up their lives; therefore God has raised them from the dead and they have entered into the victory of Christ.

You cannot kill a dead man. You cannot defeat a person who has already died. What more can you do to a man once he has died and been raised to life again?

June 20

"He Himself gave some to be apostles,
some prophets, some evangelists, and some
pastors and teachers... for the edifying of the
body of Christ, till we all come... to the measure
of the stature of the fullness of Christ."
EPHESIANS 4:11-13

Does the Body of Christ still need to be edified and encouraged? Have we all attained to the unity of the faith? Have we all obtained the full-knowledge of the Son of God? Have we all come to spiritual maturity? If the answer to all these questions is no, then these foundational ministries – ALL of them – are still needed today. And if they are still needed, then God has not withdrawn them.

June 21

"We know that the Son of God has
come and has given us an understanding,
that we may know Him..."
1 JOHN 5:20

There is a difference between salvation and a Savior; between deliverance and a Deliverer; between healing and a Healer; between redemption and a Redeemer. The first is a "thing," the second is a Person. This may sound self-evident and elementary, but before God the difference is vast, and in actual experience the difference is incalculable. If we are not clear on the matter of His Son we will find the Christian life very difficult, if not impossible, to live. I have the "thing" because I have Him; having Him, I do not need to search for the "thing" anymore. What do you have? An experience? A word? A doctrine? A belief? Or a Man? This is the difference between a living Christianity and a dead religion.

June 22

"'How hard it is for those who have
riches to enter the kingdom of God!' And the
disciples were astonished at His words. But Jesus
answered again and said to them, 'Children, how
hard it is for those who trust in riches to enter
the kingdom of God! It is easier for a camel to go
through the eye of a needle than for a rich man
to enter the kingdom of God.'"
MARK 10:23-25

The point is not that every disciple must be penniless. The point is that in this Kingdom, Christ alone has the preeminence, and you cannot serve two masters. Why are riches such a stumbling block? It all relates to Self. For the rich man, Self is mostly represented in his riches. For the wise man, Self is mostly represented in his wisdom. For the good man, Self is mostly represented in his goodness. For the strong man, Self is mostly represented in his strength.

YOU are your biggest obstacle to entering in. Why? Because there is no room in the Kingdom of God for Christ and Self.

June 23

"Now as [Paul] reasoned about righteousness,
self-control, and the judgment to come, Felix was
afraid and answered, 'Go away for now; when
I have a convenient time I will call for you.'"
ACTS 24:25

W hen the time is short we must make the most of every opportunity and waste nothing. Ordinarily if we speak the Word to someone and they send us away, the best advice is to leave. Unfortunately, Paul was in prison and could not get away. Felix sent for him often but nothing ever changed. In this manner Paul witnessed to Felix for two years without any result whatsoever. Clearly this was a ruse of the enemy designed to frustrate the gifted apostle and sap his strength.

Paul the prisoner had no choice but to come when Felix called for him; we who are free ought to be careful lest we find ourselves spending all our time talking to a Felix when there is a Cornelius praying to hear us speak the very words that Felix takes for granted.

June 24

"Put on the new man which
was created according to God, in true
righteousness and holiness."
EPHESIANS 4:24

What is the Christian Life? It is leaving our ground altogether and coming onto the ground of Christ. It is deeper than a changed life – it is an exchanged life. Over time we can accomplish a change, but we can do nothing to exchange our life for His Life. This, from start to finish, is God's work, and it is a work of grace.

What, after all, is Righteousness? What is true Holiness? Christ is not righteous because He does righteous things; He does righteous things because He is Righteousness. Christ is not holy because He does holy things; He does holy things because He is Holiness. His "doing" flows out of His "being" – and OUR "doing" flows out of His "being" as well.

June 25

"The kingdom of heaven is
like treasure hidden in a field, which a man
found and hid; and for joy over it he goes and
sells all that he has and buys that field."
MATTHEW 13:44

For too long we have contented ourselves with what God can do for us and what He can give us. We come to the Lord with a need in mind, and the next day we approach with another need, and the following day we return with yet another request. This pattern repeats itself continually. We return again and again to withdraw a little more from the heavenly bank.

Surely we should let our requests be made known unto God, and we must also ask, that we may receive. But think: if a man owns a field, does he not also possess the buried treasure in the field? Does it not stand to reason then, that if we receive HIM, we possess all He has? How shall He not, with His Son, freely give us all things?

June 26

"If anyone desires to come after Me,
let him deny himself, and take up his cross
daily, and follow Me. For whoever desires to
save his life will lose it, but whoever loses his
life for My sake will save it."
LUKE 9:23,24

Resurrection Life is that which has died, but now lives. It has the mark of the Cross upon it. It has passed through death once, and death can no more touch it. If we have not already passed through death then we are constantly fearful of dying, but the one who has already died and lives again has nothing more to fear from death. As we are decreased through the daily carrying of our cross, Christ in us is increased, and the strength of His Life is matured through our weakness.

June 27

"Your maidservant has nothing in
the house but a jar of oil."
2 KINGS 4:2

E very disciple of the Lord Jesus is at a different level of growth and spiritual maturity. But may I say that no matter how long you have walked with the Lord – be it several years or only a day – you have at least one "jar of oil" in your house.

Now what you do with that one jar of oil makes the difference between a victorious life and a defeated life. The single jar of oil is not much in and of itself. It is not sufficient to meet the demands of your creditors, nor is it sufficient to sustain your spiritual life. It is only sufficient when it is poured forth. The one who "saves" his life will lose his life, but the one who "pours out" his life will really have it in abundance.

June 28

"Thanks be to God, who gives us the
victory through our Lord Jesus Christ."
1 CORINTHIANS 15:57

Those who embrace the Cross have inherited the victory of Christ over all the works of the devil. This is the spiritual principle. The practical expression of this principle is seen when I demonstrate this victory in the battles of everyday life. If what God says about us is true, then we are not fighting *for* victory, we are fighting *from* victory – and actually, we are not fighting at all; we are merely standing in a victory that was given to us in Christ: "*Stand* therefore" (Ephesians 6:14).

June 29

"Him we preach... that we may present
every man perfect in Christ Jesus."
COLOSSIANS 1:28

The word *perfect* there means spiritually mature, having reached the full measure of the purpose for which a person is created. This, in essence, is the purpose of all ministry, whether it is the ministry of an apostle, prophet, evangelist, pastor or teacher. It is to preach Christ, and to bring all men into a spiritually mature relationship with Him.

Paul wrote to the Galatians and said they were "my little children, for whom I labor in birth again until Christ is formed in you" (Galatians 4:19). Christ was in them already, but He was not fully-formed in them yet: they were still children. Maturity in Jesus is what ministry is supposed to lead to. Christ is at the heart of everything; He is at the center of all activity; we begin with Him and we end with Him.

June 30

"'Look!' he [Nebuchadnezzar] answered,
'I see four men loose, walking in the midst of
the fire; and they are not hurt, and the form
of the fourth is like the Son of God.'"
DANIEL 3:25

O vercomers are those upon whose bodies
the fire has no power (Daniel 3:27). Put
them in the fiery furnace and they are not
consumed, only refined, only purified. It only
makes them that much more conformed to the
image of the Fourth Man, the Son of God, the
Lord Christ.

The fire has no power over them because the
fire has no power over Him, and there He is in
the midst. They do not seek the fiery furnace,
but neither do they shrink from it when it
comes. They do not ask for temptation and
testing, but they are not afraid of it. They do
not look for the devil behind every rock, but
when they find him they demonstrate the
preeminence of Christ over all things and call
for his submission to Him. This is the
Testimony of Jesus and the ministry of the
Overcomers.

July 1

"Of the increase of His government
and peace there will be no end."
ISAIAH 9:7

He MUST increase. Isaiah tells us that there will be no end of the increase of His government and peace. In the beginning was the Word, and we can see how God has worked steadily from the beginning to increase Christ. From types and shadows in the Old Testament we see Christ coming into view. Then the Word is made flesh and dwells among us, and Christ is increased yet again. Next He comes to dwell within us, and this is a major increase. Finally, He begins to conform us to His own image through His indwelling Life.

If we are growing up into Him then He is increasing daily. Eventually every knee will bow and every tongue will confess that Jesus Christ is Lord. Beyond this, we are told that God will continue to reveal His Son in the ages to come, bringing us into depths and dimensions of Christ that we cannot fathom.

July 2

"Pray then like this: 'Our Father in
heaven, hallowed be Your name.'"
MATTHEW 6:9 ESV

At once we are lifted up from the earthly
situation and are made to focus upon a
heavenly Father, a heavenly Kingdom, and a
heavenly Will. I believe it is so important for us
to see this. Prayer does not begin on the earth,
it begins in the heavens. It does not begin with
man, it begins with the Father. It does not
begin with man's need, but with God's will.

Our praying is ineffectual because we pray
as earthly men with an earthly perspective
concerning earthly things. See how far and
above this manner of praying is when
compared to the hypocrite, praying in public to
be seen of men! Prayer ought to bring us up
into the heavenlies, not bring us down deeper
into the earth. It ought to focus our vision on
the Father, not on man, or the problems of
man. Spiritual prayer begins in the Spirit;
heavenly prayer begins in the heavenlies.

July 3

"Watch and pray, lest you enter into
temptation. The spirit indeed is willing,
but the flesh is weak."
MATTHEW 26:41

The purpose of prayer is to get aligned with the Mind, Will, Heart, Desire, Purpose, and Aim of God Himself.

It is a fight and a struggle just to get to Gethsemane. It is a battle to get your siblings to stay awake with you for even one hour; and it is an all-out war to "pray thrice" or ten times or twenty times or one hundred times, as the case may be, until you have gotten the victory over yourself, and come away soaked with the blood, sweat, and tears of that early morning wrestling. But once the outcome is decided in God's favor, what awesome power and Life one receives, to drink that Cup that looked so impossible before, and to go forth bearing the Cross in the strength and power of God Himself, to do whatever He requires!

July 4

"He has delivered us from the power
of darkness and conveyed us into the kingdom
of the Son of His love."
COLOSSIANS 1:13

This Ultimate Purpose can be summed up into a single thought, a central idea, that you find weaving its way throughout the Bible and throughout human history. It is the theme of Jesus, the preaching of the apostles, and the understanding with which those first believers became followers of Christ. And this understanding of God's Ultimate Purpose and Intention finds expression in something that the Bible refers to as *The Kingdom of God*.

At the center of this Kingdom of God is a Person. Everything that God has done, is doing, and will do is centered around this Person. The Bible says that all things come from Him, through Him, and unto Him. This Person is the Lord Jesus Christ. It is God's Will that the King and His Kingdom fill all things with His Light, His Love, and His Life; and so this Kingdom is constantly growing, expanding, and increasing.

July 5

"We do not war according to the flesh."
2 CORINTHIANS 10:3

In the heat of battle it does not always seem as if the enemy is defeated. Goliath will oppose, curse, and threaten you with all sorts of taunts to convince you that you are defeated. If we listen to him long enough we will begin to doubt and this is enough to cause us to falter. We can simply ignore the lies of the enemy and stand in the truth. Our weapon of choice is the Cross. We simply return to the victory that is ours in Christ and we stand upon that finished work, and every time we do so, we demonstrate its power. Without the Cross we are naked and unprepared for facing Goliath or anything else that opposes us; but with the Cross we can no more fail than Jesus can fail.

"Not I, but Christ" defeats anything and everything that rises up to steal, kill, and destroy. It does not matter if we face Goliath, or a bad habit, or a difficult circumstance, or even the devil himself. Sooner or later, the Cross will shine forth in victory – as long as we embrace it until the very end!

July 6

"Assuredly, I say to you, whoever
does not receive the kingdom of God as a little
child will by no means enter it."
LUKE 18:17

M ake no mistake, if it is the Kingdom you
seek, the Kingdom you will find, but you
must be changed in order to enter it. If you
seek power from God you will have to accept
weakness in yourself. If you want to rule with
Him you must suffer with Him. If you want His
Life you must give up your life. You can have
either one you want, but you cannot have both.
There is no increase without decrease, and
there is no decrease without increase.

July 7

"In this manner, therefore, pray...
Your kingdom come. Your will be done
on earth as it is in heaven."
MATTHEW 6:9,10

When we pray "in this manner" we are transported and elevated beyond flesh-and-blood, beyond the natural, beyond the earthly, beyond the seen-and-felt universe in which we live. We are at once brought into alignment with Someone larger than ourselves, Someone higher, Someone greater. This Someone has an agenda, and is working all things together in one accord towards this agenda. What is the agenda? It is the Will and the Kingdom. So what is the Will and the Kingdom? The Will is "all things in Christ" and the Kingdom is the fulfillment of that Will, when Christ has the preeminence. All of God's movements are towards this End.

July 8

"Whatever gain I had, I counted as
loss for the sake of Christ."
PHILIPPIANS 3:7 ESV

The Lord will allow Self to run its due course, just like the tree whose branches fill the earth and whose height reaches to the heavens (Daniel 4:10-12). But a day of judgment is coming.

Now, those who love Self will hate judgment; but those who hate Self will love judgment. If our heart is "not I, but Christ," then we will rejoice whenever we are decreased and Christ is increased. We will submit to the Lord's dealings with us. Our focus will not be on what Self loses, but on what Christ gains, for our loss is His gain.

July 9

"The Word became flesh and dwelt
among us, and we beheld His glory, the glory as
of the only begotten of the Father,
full of grace and truth."
JOHN 1:14

Moment by moment, hour by hour, we are being changed. This transfiguration is subtle, but powerful. How is it effected? How does God change us? When we put on the Lord Jesus then we become what we have put on. When we see the glory of the Son of God then we are changed thereby. We become what we have seen.

When we see Him as He in fact is, when we behold His glory, we will be smitten to the ground. If what we have seen thus far of the Lord has not struck us dumb and blind then we have not yet touched upon His glory. Our vision is too small. May God illuminate our hearts and grant us further revelation into His Son, that we may be transfigured.

July 10

"If we walk in the light, as He is in the light, we
have fellowship with one another."
1 JOHN 1:7

True fellowship is grounded in Jesus first of all. Fellowship with others on THAT basis is neither forced, nor orchestrated; it is effortless, spontaneous, and full of Life. Fellowship naturally occurs because we have all seen and heard the same thing from the Lord – we are walking in the same Path towards Christ as All in all. We are in one accord not because we all look, think, and act just the same, but because we all, in spite of our differences, have God's End in mind.

July 11

"Thanks be to God, Who gives us the victory
through our Lord Jesus Christ."
1 CORINTHIANS 15:57

Everyone has their own way of waging warfare. Some emphasize intercessory prayer, and believe the secret is in getting hundreds of people praying for the same thing. Others lean towards praise and worship. Some stress binding and loosing. Others believe the key is in locating and naming certain spirits which supposedly control different parts of the world. Still others think there must be some prophetic act to be performed or declaration to be made.

Here is the problem with virtually all of these things: they are just that – THINGS – methods, techniques, teachings, strategies, but they are not Christ. The one in Christ is seated with Him in the heavenly places. If we see ourselves in Him then we cannot help but understand that since the battle is already won, and Victory is ours, then we do not need a method or a technique designed to "get" a victory which we already possess.

July 12

"It is the Spirit who gives life;
the flesh profits nothing."
JOHN 6:63

I f we grow impatient and fall into the flesh then we become weaker. To react in the flesh diminishes spiritual authority, and this must be avoided at all costs. Allowing the flesh to have its way for only a moment guarantees defeat against a spiritual adversary.

"We worship God in the Spirit, and rejoice in Christ Jesus, and have no confidence in the flesh" (Philippians 3:3). To lose all confidence in the flesh is to take the higher ground of the Spirit. To meet flesh with flesh means the victory will go to the strongest, and there is always someone stronger than you according to the flesh.

July 13

"The kingdoms of this world have
become the kingdoms of our Lord and of His
Christ, and He shall reign forever and ever!"
REVELATION 11:15

G od will establish an Irresistible Kingdom
on the earth. This Kingdom does not rise
up from the earth, but it comes down from
heaven. This Kingdom will break to pieces and
consume all the other kingdoms. And this
Kingdom will increase from a single Stone into
a great mountain that fills the entire earth
(Daniel 2:35). It is an Irresistible Kingdom!

Not only can this Kingdom not be stopped,
but when people see the King for Who He
really is, they no longer desire to resist Him.
This is why the Irresistible Kingdom continues
to grow and expand, so that eventually the King
and His Kingdom "fill all things."

July 14

"I do not ask that you
take them out of the world, but that
you keep them from the evil one."
John 17:15 ESV

This prayer of Jesus is answered when we embrace the Cross. The Cross renders us dead to the world so that we can bring Life to others who are in the world and not worry that we may become contaminated or polluted by the things we encounter. Jesus was not afraid of being around sinners. He affected them for good, and they were powerless to affect Him for evil. This same Jesus lives within us, and He is greater than anything we may encounter in the world. So if we are to follow His example then we must be as dead to the things of the world as He was. How is this accomplished? God's solution is for us to embrace the Cross so that we can be truly "dead" to the world's temptations and "alive" to Him. God desires a crucified people who can represent Him in the earth and be faithful to Him even in the midst of a dark, rebellious world.

July 15

"Noah... did all that God commanded him."
GENESIS 6:22 ESV

I spent many years creating and executing my own plans, asking the Lord to bless them. One day I understood that instead of always trying to get the Lord to bless what I wanted to do, it was much simpler to find out what the Lord wanted to bless, and simply do THAT. Instead of trying to get God to come down to my level and do what I wanted, it was far better to come onto the Lord's ground and do what He wanted.

Great synergy and blessing is released when we simply cooperate with what God has already purposed to do. Heaven backs us up with tremendous power and authority. Instead of trying to make something happen, I simply flow in a current that already exists. The Lord will deny no request that is in agreement with what He Himself has originated.

July 16

"I am the Way."
JOHN 14:6

What is God after? What does He seek from us? What does He want? First and foremost, He desires a people who will be conformed to the image of His Son, that they may demonstrate the preeminence of Christ in all things. But how does He gain such a people for Himself? The first step is to reveal His Son to us. This is the narrow gate. We cannot begin to walk the narrow path until we have entered the narrow gate.

Upon entering the narrow gate He begins to change us from the inside out so that it is Christ expressing Himself through us. "Not I, but Christ." This is the narrow path. This narrow path we call discipleship. It leads us somewhere. A path is not for standing still. It has a destination. Where does the path lead? What is the End? Christ as All in All. That is the End. All things work together according to this supreme purpose, His Purpose.

July 17

"Our sufficiency is from God."
2 CORINTHIANS 3:5

How will He do it? How will He demonstrate the sufficiency of His Life to do everything in your stead? Why, the next time you feel your temper getting out of control, or the person you resent is bothering you, or things are not going right, or you are tempted to quit, decide that instead of reacting the way you always do, you will trust in His Life, then stand back and just see what happens.

If you are a Christian the Life is there, it just has to be stirred up into activity. The things we call temptations, testings, and trials are the very means through which God desires to activate the Life He has placed within you! How else would we be able to rejoice in our afflictions? How else would we be able to count it all joy when we fall into many temptations and trials of faith? Humanly speaking this is impossible! But what is impossible with man is possible with God, and easily achievable when we trust in His Life to do what we cannot do.

July 18

"When He said to them, 'I am He,'
they drew back and fell to the ground."
JOHN 18:6

When they came to arrest the Lord Jesus in the garden, He asked, "Who are you looking for?" And they answered, "Jesus of Nazareth." He simply said, "I AM." When they heard this they fell over backwards to the ground. No one can stand before I AM and retain any of their strength. To the ground we will all go, for that ground is holy. Every knee will bow, and every tongue will confess that Jesus Christ is Lord.

This revealing of Christ is sufficient to bring saint and sinner alike into absolute surrender and submission. Friends and foes alike find themselves at His feet, quite unable to stand before Him. He does not have to raise His voice or call down fire from Heaven or do anything other than simply reveal Himself for Who He is. Every doubting Thomas eventually cries out, "My Lord and My God!" when they finally behold Him.

July 19

"I have been crucified with Christ;
it is no longer I who live, but Christ lives in me;
and the life which I now live in the flesh I live
by faith in the Son of God, who loved me
and gave Himself for me."
GALATIANS 2:20

The Law of Gravity brings objects to the ground. It does not matter to Gravity how large or small the object is. It works the same with acorns as it does with airplanes.

Likewise, I know today that it does not matter if I am called upon to wash dishes, mow the lawn, write an article, preach a message, cast out a demon, love my neighbor, forgive my enemy, or lay down my life. It makes no difference to the Life. It is not I, but Christ, Who does these things. The principle is the same, and the Life cannot fail. If I give up my life, if I give up my self-effort, then He begins to do what I cannot do. This is Christianity.

July 20

"A dispute arose among them as to
which of them would be greatest."
LUKE 9:46

P eter made a splendid beginning by frankly
acknowledging himself as a sinner, and so
the Lord took him just as he was and began to
disciple him.

After making some progress, however, Peter
started to lose touch with himself. He had
followed Jesus for three years and enjoyed
close fellowship with Him. He had both seen
and performed miracles in Jesus' Name. To all
outward appearances he was no longer a "sinful
man," he was a "spiritual man." Before, Peter
considered himself unworthy to be in the
presence of Jesus. In just a short period of time
you find this "sinful man" arguing along with
the other disciples about which one of them
will be the greatest!

This ought to show us that there is a deeper
death for us to die, and the more "spiritual" we
become, the more easily we are deceived by our
own spirituality.

July 21

"Whatever is born of God overcomes the world."
1 JOHN 5:4

The Overcomer demonstrates the pre-eminence of Christ over sin, self, and satan. How is preeminence demonstrated if we are still trying to fight our way to victory? We must stand in victory, not battle for it. If we do fight, we fight FROM victory, not FOR victory. It must be to us an accomplished fact, not a future hope, and just there lies the difference between those who are still waging warfare and those who are quietly resting in Christ and steadily praying His Will into the earth.

July 22

"'The stone which the builders rejected
has become the chief cornerstone,' and 'A stone
of stumbling and a rock of offense.'"
1 PETER 2:7,8

The people to whom Jesus preached already had their own ideas about what the Messiah would do, and what His Kingdom would look like. Unfortunately those ideas were utterly wrong. So Jesus said they needed to repent: to change their heart, to change their mind, to change their behavior, and to get ready to experience something that went totally against their preconceived ideas and notions.

To enter the Kingdom of God and to know the King around which this Kingdom is organized requires a radical change on many levels. The way you perceive things, the way you relate to things, the way you understand things – all of it has to be changed. At the very least it must be challenged.

July 23

"Stir up the gift of God which is in you
through the laying on of my hands. For God has
not given us a spirit of fear, but of power and of
love and of a sound mind. Therefore do not be
ashamed of the testimony of our Lord."
2 TIMOTHY 1:6-8

Paul does not tell Timothy to pray for a better opportunity, or passively wait for God to rise up within him and overwhelm him. Timothy needed to exercise the gift. He needed to stir it up. He had something to offer, something to contribute.

Paul's exhortation was not to persist in false humility or passive waiting, but to be proactive, to stir it up, and serve the Body of Christ as a faithful steward. According to Paul's assessment, it was not a spirit of humility that held Timothy back, it was a spirit of fear.

July 24

"But of Him you are in Christ Jesus,
who became for us wisdom from God—
and righteousness and sanctification
and redemption."
1 CORINTHIANS 1:30

This is a very rich verse. We have already seen how the Lord Jesus is given to be our Life. Upon that basis we can lay claim to everything else. Here we see that to those of us who are in Christ, He is made to be our wisdom, righteousness, sanctification, and redemption. It does not say that He gives these things to us, but that He *is* these things *in* us.

July 25

"This Gospel of the Kingdom will be
preached in all the world as a witness to all the
nations; and then the end will come."
MATTHEW 24:14

W hy does the Lord delay His return? Not
for any lack of desire on His part to
consummate His Kingdom, but because of His
great love, and His compassion for all. Peter
says He is not willing that any should perish,
but that all should come to repentance. We
have noted how the Gospel of the Kingdom is
rarely preached today. Perhaps God is
revealing this to His people yet again, re-
emphasizing it to the Ekklesia so it can be
proclaimed to all nations as His last invitation
before the end of this age.

The fact that we do not know when He will
return, the fact that we are to be ready at all
times, means there is nothing to prevent Him
from coming today. The next great event in the
recovery of the Heavenly Order is the return of
the King.

July 26

"Indeed I also count all things loss for the
excellence of the knowledge of Christ Jesus my
Lord, for whom I have suffered the loss of all
things, and count them as rubbish,
that I may gain Christ."
PHILIPPIANS 3:8

For the Christian, Christ is increasing, Christ is becoming larger and larger, Christ is becoming the focus. It is quite simple to see who is, and who is not, living up to this standard.

The more spiritually mature a person is the more Christ-centered they cannot help but become. This is the unavoidable and inevitable consequence of becoming a Christian, a disciple of Jesus. This is how the Holy Spirit leads each and every true believer, and there are no exceptions to the rule. It is as predictable and certain as the sunrise following after the darkness of night.

July 27

"I sought for a man among them who
would make a wall, and stand in the gap before
Me on behalf of the land, that I should not
destroy it; but I found no one."
EZEKIEL 22:30

T he Lord searches the whole Earth, and
when He has found a person who sees that
Purpose, and daily orders their life according to
that Purpose, and (here is the key!) consistently
rises up to pray for the fulfillment of that
Purpose, then God will move Heaven and Earth
on behalf of that person; for He has found, at
last, some ground to build upon.

That person is numbered with the Remnant
because, I promise you, men and women like
that are few and far between.

July 28

"Pilate said to Him, 'What is truth?'"
JOHN 18:38

We are often unprepared for Truth, which is why Truth is revealed to us progressively. We must "grow up into Him" – we could not handle it otherwise. Even the little bit of Truth which is revealed to us often upsets us at our deepest foundations. We must be willing to live with the uncertainty and pain which Truth brings. But if we accept the Truth, and totally give ourselves to it, it will begin to change us. We will begin to be conformed to it, and it will become less painful.

I am convinced that if we refuse to accept the Truth we have been given then we will eventually lose it. This is why some grow spiritually and some do not. Even though they may acknowledge the same Truth, they may not be willing to accept the consequences of being transformed by that Truth, thus what little they have soon becomes dead manna.

July 29

"Put on the new man which
was created according to God, in true
righteousness and holiness."
EPHESIANS 4:24

The old man (self) is put off, and the New Man (Christ) is put on – this is Christianity. Christ then becomes my Righteousness and my Holiness. But too many of us take a natural, intellectual approach to Christianity. We think if only we can instruct people concerning the tenets of our faith, or persuade them with a logical argument, or woo them with some emotional plea, then we will have disciples. This is a falsehood. That is not Spirit and Life.

Christianity is not memorizing certain doctrines or disseminating a systematic theology or having people repeat a so-called "Sinner's Prayer." Christianity is becoming one with a God-Man! You can have all the other in its proper place, but for too long that "other" has been offered as Christianity. And so people touch our beliefs, our doctrines, our religion, our theology, our zeal, but they do not touch a Living Christ.

July 30

"He who does not take his cross and follow
after Me is not worthy of Me."
MATTHEW 10:38

A re you worthy of the Lord Jesus Christ?
Hear what the Lord is saying here. "If you
do not take up your Cross and follow Me, you
do not deserve Me."

It is not merely a question of are we
following Christ. The crux of the matter is: have
we taken up the Cross? There is an order to this
call to become disciples of Jesus Christ: first,
we must take up our Cross; only then may we
follow after Him. It is not, "first follow Me, and
later take your Cross." The Cross is step one.
Our taking up the Cross is basic to our
following Christ, not something we are called to
do after many years. The so-called "deeper
Christian life" is but the normal Christian life.
Anything less is abnormal. There is no greater
depth to the Christian life but what God
expects of all of us from the beginning. If we
are getting any "deeper" it is only because we
have hitherto been shallow. We must take our
Cross and follow Jesus.

July 31

"If I have told you earthly things
and you do not believe, how will you believe
if I tell you heavenly things?"
JOHN 3:12

The path of progress, of spiritual maturity, hinges upon our willingness to let go of the old ways and embrace the new ways; to rise above the lower order of things and walk in a higher order – a heavenly way, a spiritual way, as opposed to the earthly, natural, carnal way that we are so used to walking. Repentance is a continual process of agreeing with what God shows us about ourselves and then making the necessary adjustments.

The Holy Spirit is intent upon making radical adjustments – to create in us a willingness to look at things differently; an eagerness to begin seeing things as God sees them, regardless of how uncomfortable that may be; to value the things that He values and let go of lesser things; to align ourselves with His Mind and Will for all things; to leave our ground altogether and come onto His ground – regardless of the consequences.

August 1

"When they had lifted up their eyes,
they saw no one but Jesus only."
MATTHEW 17:8

W hen we SEE an ever-increasing Christ Who is destined to fill all things, then we will be delivered from smallness and narrow-mindedness. We do not overcome a thing by focusing our attention and directing our energies against that THING. "Things" will keep us busy from morning until night, and from night until morning.

May God deliver us from "things" and show us His Son! We must learn to keep the focus of our heart on the Lord Jesus Christ, Who MUST increase. Then there is no room for "things" anymore. They are simply swallowed up in Victory.

August 2

"God is able to make all grace
abound toward you."
2 CORINTHIANS 9:8

G od will not LEAD you where His grace cannot KEEP you. That is to say, when we undertake the work assigned to us by the Lord we will find the Life of the Lord is present to give us all the inner spiritual strength to see it through to completion.

I am not saying everything will go smoothly and you will never have any self-doubt or fear. Far from it. But listen to what Paul says: "We are hard-pressed on every side, yet not crushed; we are perplexed, but not in despair; persecuted, but not forsaken; struck down, but not destroyed" (2 Corinthians 4:8,9). His secret? "I also labor, striving according to His working which works in me mightily" (Colossians 1:29). Not I, but Christ. This is the secret to the Christian life and it is the key to all fruitful spiritual work.

August 3

"He must increase."
JOHN 3:30

God is not moving backward, but in the Son and through the Son, He moves steadily forward. Christ MUST increase. This is the Law of the Spirit of Life in Christ Jesus.

Just as we cannot have gravity without having the law of gravity, so it is impossible to have the Life of the Lord but not have the Law of that Life. And the Law of Life is that Christ must increase.

August 4

"Do not fear, for those who are with us are
more than those who are with them."
2 KINGS 6:16

E lisha saw differently, and so he thought, spoke, and behaved differently. So often we try to adopt a certain way of thinking, speaking, and acting in hopes of becoming victorious. If this is your intention then you are already defeated. If victory lies in something you must do then you will never be able to do enough. "Acting spiritual" does not produce victory, for victory is not what I do or do not do: Victory is Christ.

August 5

"Do not fear, Daniel, for from
the first day that you set your heart to
understand, and to humble yourself before
your God, your words were heard."
DANIEL 10:12

D aniel prevailed over Earth because he was of Heaven. Daniel prevailed over Darkness because he was of the Light. Daniel prevailed over Death because he had Life. Daniel was delivered from the lion's den, and lived to continue his ministry of prayer. After such an ordeal we might expect him to go ahead and retire, to quietly settle down, and relax a little bit. Certainly he has earned a vacation. But shortly thereafter we find him battling in the spirit for twenty-one days while he waited for yet another answer to be delivered from Heaven. Can there be any doubt as to the outcome?

Daniel does not stop. This is what it means to overcome. You can never coast, you can never let down your guard, you can never just let things slide for a day or two. Overcoming is not a once in awhile thing, it is an all-the-time thing. Settle that within yourself right now.

August 6

"He turned to His disciples and said
privately, 'Blessed are the eyes which see the
things you see; for I tell you that many prophets
and kings have desired to see what you see,
and have not seen it, and to hear what
you hear, and have not heard it.'"
LUKE 10:23,24

The object of Christianity is not to give people a teaching or to lead them in a prayer, but to introduce them to a Man. I would rather have thirty seconds of seeing than thirty years of preaching. People can listen to me preach all their life and never understand a word, but if the Lord opens their eyes to SEE Who I am preaching about then they will understand everything.

August 7

"We walk by faith, not by sight."
2 CORINTHIANS 5:7

The question for us remains: what do we see? Many people look, but do not see. They look at the world and believe everything it says. Others have their eyes opened to see as the Lord sees. This revelation, or unveiling, is what enables us to live in the world while being apart from the world. This seeing enables us to overcome the world and demonstrate Christ as All in All. We do not have to live according to what we see or feel, but according to the Law of the Spirit of Life in Christ.

May God show us who we are, and may God raise us up to walk worthy of the calling He has given us.

August 8

"Blessed are the merciful,
for they shall obtain mercy."
MATTHEW 5:7

God is "rich in mercy" (Ephesians 2:4). Entry into His Kingdom is established upon the principles of grace, mercy, and forgiveness. To live in His Kingdom is to experience the grace, mercy, and forgiveness of God on a daily basis. The nature of the Kingdom reflects the character of its King. If this is so, how can we claim to be representatives of this Kingdom of Love and refuse to forgive as freely as we have been forgiven? If we have been forgiven by God then we have an obligation to forgive others – not for their sake, not for our sake, but for the sake of the Kingdom.

It would be inconceivable to claim to be a king and priest of a Kingdom based on forgiveness of sins and, at the same time, allow unforgiveness and bitterness to remain in our personal life. It will be difficult for people to believe God can forgive them if His own people are unable or unwilling to forgive one another.

August 9

"He put all in subjection under Him, He left nothing that is not put under Him. But now we do not yet see all things put under Him."

HEBREWS 2:8

Even though Jesus is Lord, not everyone recognizes that, appreciates it, or acknowledges it. Our adversary the devil still walks around as a roaring lion seeking whom he may devour (1 Peter 5:8). That there exists some spiritual force that continues in active resistance to Christ is proof enough that we do not yet see all things put under Him.

We also note the presence of sin, poverty, disease, death, and evil as being very much a part of the world in which we live. So there is still much to be done in terms of putting all things beneath Him. But the presence of the word "yet" should inspire us and fill us with hope! Although we do not *yet* see all things put under Him, the word "yet" implies that eventually we *will* see all things put under Him. That is to say, in due course, God's Purpose will be fulfilled, and we will see all things put under Him – even though we do not "yet" see it.

August 10

"The Revelation of Jesus Christ..."
REVELATION 1:1

The Book of Revelation itself is not primarily the revelation of what the end of the world will be like (although we do learn that), but is the Revelation and Testimony of Jesus Christ. We are immediately confronted with a vision of Jesus Christ standing in the midst of the Ekklesia: it is quite different from the image of the suffering Messiah, despised and rejected of men. So, this is a further unveiling or revealing of the Lord Jesus and is genuinely prophetic.

The rest of the book, its symbols, and its meaning may be unclear, and we may disagree with the interpretations thereof, but the main gist of the book, the revealing of Jesus Christ as the King of Kings and the Lord of Lords, the Alpha and the Omega, the Beginning and the End, the First and the Last, is beyond dispute.

August 11

"It came to pass, as He sat at the
table with them, that He took bread, blessed and
broke it, and gave it to them. Then their eyes
were opened and they knew Him; and He
vanished from their sight."
LUKE 24:30,31

After Jesus blessed the bread, and broke it, and gave it to them, their eyes were opened and they knew Him. Until you have the blessing and the breaking your eyes will remain closed. Blessings alone do not open our eyes. Indeed, blessings by themselves tend to close our eyes. We do not come to know Him in the blessing, but in the breaking. Then what we already have in Him will be revealed. Our eyes will be opened and we will see that He has been standing there the whole time.

Do you want to know Him? Do you want to see Him for Who He is? Do you want to go deeper? Do you want to have your eyes opened? Embrace the blessing AND the breaking; receive them both. If you are a bruised reed or a broken cistern, take heart, because you are making progress.

August 12

"All who desire to live a godly life in
Christ Jesus will be persecuted."
2 TIMOTHY 3:12 ESV

P ersecution should come as no surprise to those who seek first the Kingdom of God, because that kind of single-hearted pursuit for things Above will only antagonize those earthly-minded folk who cannot comprehend that level of Righteousness where Jesus is really All and Everything.

Persecution for the sake of that all-encompassing Righteousness, that universal dominion of Christ on His Throne, is the best proof we could possibly give that we really are kings and priests. The depth of our sufferings reveals the depth of our relationship with God, and if our suffering is light then our relationship is certainly shallow. When we can take up the Cross daily and follow after Christ then the centurions of this world will be able to look at us and say, "Surely this person is a son or daughter of God. Not only do they represent Him with their life, they represent Him with their death."

August 13

"If we say that we have fellowship
with Him, and walk in darkness, we lie and
do not practice the truth."
1 JOHN 1:6

Overcomers are learning to bridge the gap between what they SAY they believe and how they really LIVE.

The one that overcomes is constantly challenging the lie of the enemy and demonstrating the preeminence of Christ over all things. When every lie is destroyed then the dragon is defeated, for it cannot control what it cannot deceive.

Most of what we see and hear is an illusion. It is not the Truth, but a lie, a distortion. Our eyes and our ears cannot be trusted. We must have heavenly vision and heavenly hearing.

August 14

"He will guide you into all truth."
JOHN 16:13

S ince Jesus is the Truth, the Holy Spirit will lead us into all truth by increasing Christ. The Scriptures that tell us about Jesus are inspired by the Holy Spirit. The ability to understand those Scriptures is given by the Holy Spirit. The fruit that comes from abiding in Jesus is the result of the Holy Spirit.

If you learn anything concerning Jesus and His Irresistible Kingdom by reading this book it will not be because of me. My ability to write is a gift of the Holy Spirit so that Christ will be increased; likewise, your ability to read and comprehend what is written is a gift of the Holy Spirit. And when I stop writing, and you stop reading, and we go forth to put into practice what we have learned, we will do so by, through, and because of the Holy Spirit, Whom the Father has given, to lead us and guide us deeper into Christ.

August 15

"A disciple is not above his teacher,
nor a servant above his master."
MATTHEW 10:24

J esus said go into all the world and make disciples. It is not that ministers and workers are unimportant; indeed they are. But what is the priority? Can a man or a woman truly be a minister or worker on behalf of the Kingdom if they are not a disciple first? Of course not. They can minister and work themselves to death and still be in the flesh, doing many mighty works in the name of Jesus and not know Him at all.

August 16

"We wanted to come to you—even I, Paul,
time and again—but Satan hindered us."
1 THESSALONIANS 2:18

I f we will wait patiently before the Lord then He will make us know His will. Almost any mistake can be rectified except presumption and rashness. The flesh is always in a hurry, so we should begin to equate "getting in a hurry" with "getting in the flesh." Out of one thousand presumptuous acts, nine hundred and ninety-nine of them are flesh.

We want instant relief, instant answers, and instant results, but God wants us to slow down, remain calm, be still, and know that He is God. He wants us to apprehend His Mind, wait for His Spirit, and become acquainted with His ways.

August 17

"He must increase, but I must decrease."
JOHN 3:30

A disciple of the Lord Jesus is someone who enters the narrow gate and walks the narrow path until they come to the end of the narrow path and are left with nothing but Christ. As you can see, this is a very, very narrow way, which is why few find it, and fewer still remain on it once they find it. Nothing of self can be retained. All of self must be lost in order to gain Christ.

As we walk the narrow way we are being changed from glory to glory. Today we should reflect a little more of the glory of God than yesterday; tomorrow we will reflect yet more than we did today. This is growth. Growth is not more knowledge or increase of years: it is simply more of Him and less of me. He increases as I decrease. This is what it means to be a disciple.

August 18

"The things which are impossible with men
are possible with God."
LUKE 18:27

Once God has determined to do something, is there anything, or anyone, that can resist Him? Is man more powerful than God, or does it only seem that way sometimes? It does appear that God, in His infinite wisdom and loving-kindness and patience, chooses to delay the fulfillment of His Will. Man can try to withstand it, the devil can rebel against it, and by collaborating with man can even appear to hinder and prevent it temporarily – but in the end, God will have His Will.

Let no one mistake God's longsuffering for any inability to bring about His desire and accomplish His Purpose. His plan is unavoidable and irresistible.

August 19

"To this end I also labor,
striving according to His working
which works in me mightily."
COLOSSIANS 1:29

The one who rests in Christ will produce more fruit than the one who strives with self-effort. This is demonstrated in Scripture and in the real-life experience of countless saints.

There is no question that Paul worked, labored, and toiled. But the difference with Paul is he knew that he was laboring according to Christ working in him. Was Paul lazy? By contrast, he was more fruitful than ever. The end result is his statement, "I labored more abundantly than them all," quickly qualified with, "yet not I, but the grace of God which was with me" (1 Corinthians 15:10). The "I can do all things" must always be followed with "through Christ Who strengthens me." If we trust in the Life we will be anything but passive.

August 20

"Be strengthened with might through
His Spirit in the inner man, that Christ may dwell
in your hearts through faith; that you, being
rooted and grounded in love, may be able
to comprehend with all the saints what is the
width and length and depth and height."
EPHESIANS 3:16-18

We have to come to know the breadth, length, depth, and height of HIM, and may I say that we will never come to the end of Him. But we do not search for anything as if we do not have it, nor do we hope to gain some new thing, for what we call "new" is simply that which has been seen for the first time. Thus, revelation is critical, for it unveils what we already have. Having the Son, we have All.

August 21

"If you are led by the Spirit, you are
not under the law. If we live in the Spirit,
let us also walk in the Spirit."
GALATIANS 5:18,25

I n the wilderness you don't follow your feelings. It says the children of Israel were led by a column of smoke by day and a pillar of fire by night. When the cloud moved then they moved. When the cloud stayed still then they stayed still. I mean it's really as simple as that.

Walk in the Spirit. If you begin to be led by your feelings then you'll make the wrong decision every time. Most of the time, the right decision doesn't feel good. Doing the right thing is usually difficult. The easiest thing to do is to quit, to give up, to go back to Egypt. But I'm telling you, get to the place where going back is no longer an option – then going back is no longer a temptation.

August 22

"The Lord is my shepherd;
I shall not want. You anoint my head with
oil; my cup runs over."
PSALM 23:1,5

An anointed head and a cup that runs over – this is the hallmark of the Christian. An anointed head exudes a heavenly fragrance that sets us apart from the world, even though we walk about in it daily. It is bearing the Testimony of Jesus that witnesses of a heavenly reality that is quite distinct from the earthly fact. The cup that runs over means we have an ample supply of the Life of the Lord. If we can contain ourselves then we have yet to touch the Lord. For once we have indeed touched the Lord we will overflow. We will not be able to contain Him.

All who walk with the Shepherd should experience Infinite Supply: a never-ending flow of the Life, Light, and Love of the Lord Jesus Himself. This is the normal Christian life, and it is God's provision for every disciple.

August 23

"My yoke is easy, and My burden is light."
MATTHEW 11:30

The Law of Life is more powerful and active than anything generated or maintained by self-effort. With self-effort I am always at the mercy of how I feel. If I feel spiritual then I can pray for hours at a time. But if I do not feel spiritual then I cannot even pray for five minutes.

This is why so many believers live their lives like a roller-coaster. They do not live according to principle, according to the Law of Life. Thinking it is up to them to become Christ-like, they turn an easy yoke and a light burden into a difficult yoke and a heavy burden – difficult and heavy for themselves, and for those who must live and work around them. The one who rests in Christ will produce more fruit than the one who strives with self-effort.

August 24

"When the Son of Man comes, will
He really find faith on the earth?"
LUKE 18:8

This is perhaps one of the most intriguing questions Jesus ever put forth – from a human perspective it almost sounds as if He wonders about it Himself. There is no doubt that He will perform what He has promised to us; but will we perform what we have promised to Him? Can we patiently wait for Him to fulfill His Word, no matter how long it takes?

Rest assured that, "Now our salvation is nearer than when we first believed" (Romans 13:11). Two thousand years after His promise we are even closer to its fulfillment.

August 25

"Do you not know that he who is joined
to a harlot is one body with her? For 'the two,'
He says, 'shall become one flesh.' But he who is
joined to the Lord is one spirit with Him."
1 CORINTHIANS 6:16,17

O ne theme that constantly appears in Scripture is the believer's spiritual union with Christ. This joining together is perfectly pictured in the illustration of the Ekklesia as the Bride of Christ. When Paul wished to encourage the Corinthians to "flee fornication," he made a similar analogy but from a very different perspective.

The physical joining together of man and woman, whether in marriage or outside of marriage, has the effect of making them one flesh. Spiritually speaking, the Bride of Christ is joined to the Lord and is now one spirit with Him. This is an admittedly difficult point to get across – even Paul said this is a great mystery, and you do not usually find him to be at a loss for words when it comes to explaining something.

August 26

"Let no one despise your youth, but be an
example to the believers in word, in conduct, in
love, in spirit, in faith, in purity."
1 TIMOTHY 4:12

An older person is not necessarily a spiritual elder. We do not look to the age of a person's physical body when determining their spiritual maturity. Of course, we owe a certain amount of respect to the aged by virtue of their seniority; but they may not necessarily be our elder in the things of the Lord.

One can be older chronologically and be quite immature in spiritual matters. Likewise, a relatively young man or woman can have a deep relationship with the Lord and be light years ahead of those two or three times their age. A young man or woman who knows God is more elder than a senior citizen who does not know God. We cannot judge by the flesh, or we will be misled.

August 27

"The message of the cross... to us who are
being saved, it is the power of God."
1 CORINTHIANS 1:18

It does not matter what your situation is; the Cross is sufficient. If the Cross is the power of God for salvation, then the Cross is also the power of God for your relationships, your spiritual growth and development, your life's purpose, your encouragement and strength, and your victory over everything which hinders and distracts and comes against you. At one time in your life you learned you could not save yourself – that was the work of the Cross.

Now, accept the work of the Cross and learn that just as you could not save yourself, neither can you love God, love your neighbor, forgive those who have sinned against you, cast out devils, be a bold witness for Christ, or fulfill your destiny in your own strength. Just as you once relied upon Christ to save you, so now you must rely upon Christ to live through you every day. Just as you continually rely upon Christ for salvation, so you must continually rely upon Christ for everything else.

August 28

"My God shall supply all your need
according to His riches in glory by Christ Jesus."
PHILIPPIANS 4:19

We need more than a touch from God; we must have God Himself. There is an ocean of difference between receiving the blessing and receiving the One Who blesses; between getting a touch and receiving the One Who touches; between healing and the Healer; between redemption and Redeemer; between salvation and Savior. The former deals with what God has or can do, while the latter deals with God Himself.

August 29

"When you are old, you will stretch out your
hands, and Another will dress you and carry you
where you do not want to go."
JOHN 21:18 ESV

One characteristic of young disciples is their ability to dress and lead themselves. They find it very easy to go out and to come in. They are zealous and full of good works.

We are not suggesting that this is necessarily wrong, but we are suggesting that this is only the beginning stage of spiritual growth. The real question is not what need do I want to fill, or where do I want to go, or what do I want to say, or what do I want to do. The question is: what glorifies the Lord? Whenever "I" do something I consider spiritual and good, it is, nevertheless, "me" who does it.

Often we do what glorifies us – the Lord and His Need are seldom considered. But when we ask what glorifies the Lord, we see (in this passage at least) that the Lord is glorified when He is able to dress us and lead us where HE wants us to go – with no interference from Self.

August 30

"I have given them Your word; and the
world has hated them because they are not of
the world, just as I am not of the world."
JOHN 17:14

When we are called to put on the New Man
we are challenged with something
radical, something which by reason of Who He
is must result in an upsetting of the natural,
earthly order of things. It is a major upheaval.
Why? Because this New Man is Totally Other.
This New Man is of Heaven. This New Man is
Spirit. This New Man is foreign from this
world.

And when we put on THIS New Man, we are
going to be at once set apart from the world
and earmarked for something larger than we
can fathom with our mind, something apart
from flesh and blood, something we call "Spirit
and Life."

August 31

"He who does not take his cross and follow
after Me is not worthy of Me."
MATTHEW 10:38

It is unfortunate that after many years of service the Lord still has to call us back to the Cross, yet this is precisely where we should have begun. Although we ought to encourage people to come as they are and trust the Lord for salvation, we must also teach them that they must count the cost and take up the Cross: else they are not worthy of Jesus! God cannot fill us until He empties us. The Cross is where we are poured out that He may pour in.

September 1

"I am the light of the world."
JOHN 8:12

M any people write to me and ask how to deal with this thing or that, how to get the victory here or there. May I say that it does not matter what your need is, or what your problem is, the Answer is the same. Victory is a *Man*, not an experience. If you must fail a hundred, a thousand, or a million times in order to learn that lesson then it is worth it.

It does not matter whether you understand it, agree with it, believe it, or see it yet. Indeed, everything else seems to say the opposite. But you will see, just as I have seen, that Victory, Grace, Strength, Peace, Love, Light, and Life are not "things," they are Christ, and having the Man, you have everything the Man is.

September 2

"Called... out of darkness
into His marvelous Light."
1 PETER 2:9

T he significant thing to be seen in Creation (and the encouraging thing to us spiritually) is that God, being God, could not and would not, permit this chaos, confusion, and darkness to continue indefinitely. His nature is to bring order, coherency, purposeful intention, and Light into the world.

We owe our physical life to the fact that God acted upon the chaos that existed in Genesis 1 and commanded Light to come forth. And we owe our spiritual life to the fact that God acts upon the chaos and darkness of our lives and commands His Light to come forth. The calling forth of Light out of Darkness is a spiritual principle that teaches us the ways of God. See how He sets aside Darkness with only a single command: "Let there be Light." It is even more simple in the Hebrew: "Light: BE!" And so it was.

September 3

"It pleased the Father that in Him
all the fullness should dwell."
COLOSSIANS 1:19

He must increase; therefore, He will increase, and He is increasing. It must be so, therefore it is so. It is so simple. He must increase. Why? Because God has ordained that Christ must have the preeminence in all things. He clearly does not have that preeminence in all things now; and so, He must increase until He does have the preeminence in all things.

This is a Universal Spiritual Principle because it is at work right now. Whether you believe it or not, whether you understand it or not, whether you like it or not; the Bible says it must be, and so it is.

September 4

"When John had heard in prison about
the works of Christ, he sent two of his disciples
and said to Him, 'Are You the Coming One,
or do we look for another?'"
MATTHEW 11:2,3

Have you discovered Him yet, and is He enough, or do you look for another? We do not proclaim the preeminence of Christ because it is a nice doctrine to believe in; for us, it is a matter of life and death, because everything hinges on whether or not Jesus is preeminent. If He is preeminent then He is Enough, and there is nothing else but Him, and there is nothing worth proclaiming except Him.

To John in prison, and to us wherever we may happen to be, Jesus says, "No, you did not make a mistake. I am the One, but I am more than you can imagine, more than you dare to dream. Blessed are they who are not offended in Me."

September 5

"While they were talking and discussing together,
Jesus himself drew near and went with them. But
their eyes were kept from recognizing him."
LUKE 24:15,16 ESV

You see that Christ is revealed or hidden from men as He so desires. So many professed disciples of the Lord Jesus fail to recognize Him.

Even His closest disciples are prone to doubt and unbelief. After the resurrection, Thomas declared, "I will not believe unless I see the scars and put my hand into the wound in His side." When Jesus therefore appeared to them He did not argue or try to convince Thomas. He simply said, "Look! See My hands and My feet!" When Thomas saw the Lord, he spontaneously cried out, "My Lord, and my God!" This is revelation. Revelation does not require any arguing or convincing, as if it all depends on how well we can make a defense of the Gospel. I see no argument in the Lord Jesus, I only see Him. Seeing Him, I am convinced, and no argument is necessary.

September 6

"Daniel purposed in his heart
that he would not defile himself with
the portion of the king's delicacies, nor with
the wine which he drank."
DANIEL 1:8

T he easiest thing to do is to just go along with things, accept them as they are, and not make any trouble. But thank God for that decision! Daniel purposed in his heart – a flame was kindled, and the longer he thought about it, the hotter the fire burned.

While the others were eating and drinking, Daniel motioned to his three friends, and whispered, "Eat mine if you will have it – but I will not sin against the Lord in this thing!" And the three brothers, Hananiah, Mishael, and Azariah, agreed that they would not eat the meat or drink the wine either. Hallelujah! This is what the Lord is after – a small company of two or three, gathered together under a covenant that they will stand for the Testimony of the Lord, for something Heavenly, regardless of the cost!

September 7

"You seek Me, not because you saw the signs, but
because you ate of the loaves and were filled."
JOHN 6:26

The ones who seek bread from the Lord will be temporarily filled, but all who seek the Lord as Bread will be constantly satisfied. What is more, they will have resources from which to feed others.

It is a shame that many Christians only seek to be filled, and still they are never satisfied. They are content with a meager pittance, for a few crumbs from the table (Mark 7:28). They are constantly obsessed with being filled. To such ones we can only say that it is time to seek the Lord, not for what He can give you, but for Himself.

September 8

"What does the Lord require of you
but to do justly, to love mercy, and to walk
humbly with your God?"
MICAH 6:8

According to Vines Expository Dictionary of Bible Words, "Mercy is the outward manifestation of pity; it assumes need on the part of him who receives it, and resources adequate to meet the need on the part of him who shows it."

Ideally, forgiveness is based on repentance; but whether or not a person repents and asks for forgiveness, they are still in need of mercy (even if they do not deserve it). If nothing else, we can pray that a merciful God will open their eyes and show them their true condition. The question is not whether or not someone deserves mercy, but whether or not they need mercy, and whether or not my spiritual life is rich enough to extend it to them.

September 9

"The Lamb will overcome them,
for He is Lord of lords and King of kings;
and those who are with Him are
called, chosen, and faithful."
REVELATION 17:14

The Lord is calling out for Overcomers, those who have the Revelation of Christ and who bear the Testimony of Jesus; those who demonstrate the preeminence of Christ over all things. That is your purpose as a Christian – in fact, it has always been God's purpose for saving you and leaving you on the earth, whether you have realized it or not. You are NOT on the earth to be constantly disappointed, discouraged, and defeated. You are on the earth to demonstrate the preeminence of Christ; to show the world that "the heavens do rule."

A defeated Christian is a contradiction: it is not your destiny. Rise up and live according to the truth: that Victory is a Man, and He lives inside of you, and the One Who lives within you is greater than whatever comes against you.

September 10

"You are of God, little children, and have overcome them, because He who is in you is greater than he who is in the world."
1 JOHN 4:4

John declares that no matter what comes against us, the One within us is Greater. It does not matter what you feel like, what you see, what you hear, what people say, or what the devil does. It does not matter if Lazarus is dead for four days and is beginning to stink. It does not matter if the girl dies before Jesus can get there. It does not matter if the waves are about to capsize the boat. It does not matter if Paul is stoned and left for dead. Lazarus will be raised, the girl will be brought back to life, and the storm will be silenced, and Paul will preach again.

The Greater is always Greater, and the Lesser is always Lesser. We only have a problem when we see everything else as "greater" and see Christ as "lesser."

September 11

"By grace you have been saved
through faith, and that not of yourselves;
it is the gift of God, not of works,
lest anyone should boast."
EPHESIANS 2:8,9

When you come to the Lord Jesus for the first time, regardless of the circumstances, it means that on some level you have come to the realization that you cannot save yourself, that salvation is only possible through Him. No one seeks a Savior if they believe they can still save themselves. Only when you realize that you cannot save yourself will you acknowledge your need for Someone Else to do the saving. This is usually not the result of some intellectual argument or emotional plea, but the cold hard reality one faces after having tried unsuccessfully to do everything on their own.

We may fail once, twice, a dozen times, a hundred times. But when we finally surrender to God we are decreased, and He is increased. Practically speaking it simply means a little less confidence and faith in yourself, and a little more confidence and faith in Christ.

September 12

"He chose us in Him before the foundation of the
world... according to the purpose of His will."
EPHESIANS 1:4,5 ESV

God is not random. He doesn't act without a Purpose, without a Plan, without some big Universal Goal. He is not haphazard or accidental. As much as a writer envisions the completed book before he begins to write it, and as much as the artist envisions the portrait in her head before she begins to paint it, God sees what He wants and "all things work together for good... according to His Purpose" (Romans 8:28). Creation bears witness to a purposeful, intentional Creator and so do we. Just as the days of Creation unfold and we see a progressive revelation of the heart, intention, purpose, mind, and will of God taking shape in Creation, you can rest assured that through successive ages God is bringing about His Will, not just in the physical world, but in the spiritual world.

September 13

"Suddenly a great light from heaven
shone around me. And I fell to the ground and
heard a voice saying to me, 'Saul, Saul, why
are you persecuting Me?'"
ACTS 22:6,7

All it takes is a millisecond of time for the Revelation to strike you down. I recall when I first received the Revelation of Jesus Christ. I had had many religious and spiritual experiences up to that point, more than the average person. I had been a pastor and teacher for many years. I thought I really knew the Lord. But one day God revealed His Son IN me. I was sitting in the backyard reading the Word and without warning, in my heart of hearts, I "saw" (not with my eyes, but inwardly) Jesus seated at God's right hand, and I saw myself raised and seated with Him in heavenly places (Ephesians 2:6).

That day was like walking out of one room and into another, closing the door behind me. I got a glimpse into another world. I saw the real Jesus and realized He was nothing like flesh and blood had said. Hallelujah!

September 14

"Our old man was crucified with Him."
ROMANS 6:6

Thank God for the Cross of Jesus Christ! For it is there that my sins are forgiven; it is there that the "old man" died. Yet it is also true that there is something as wicked, if not more wicked, than sin, and that is Self. It is true that every sin is rooted in Self.

As we must initially accept His death for sin, so we must daily accept our death to Self. As we are once crucified with Him for the remission of sins, so we must daily take up the Cross, deny our Self, and follow Him. We walk in the narrow Way just as we entered the narrow Gate – by way of the Cross.

September 15

"Do not worry about tomorrow."
MATTHEW 6:34

Most of us, from time to time or nearly all of the time, worry about something – our health, our finances, our loved ones, and so on. Yet the Scriptures say to take no thought for your lives and be anxious for nothing. Why is worry a sin? I know we consider it "only human," but worry really implies a lack of trust in God. It is believing a lie. Identify the lie and you can quickly discover the Truth. What is the lie? That God is somehow less than sufficient, that perhaps He will not come through for us.

So you see, the enemy gets us to believe a lie, and then gets us to think that we are just being "human." So then we accept something less than the normal Christian life – overcoming – and think that is just the way it is. Remember: satan has no power apart from our belief in his lie.

September 16

"Cast out this slave woman with her
son, for the son of this slave woman shall not
be heir with my son Isaac."
GENESIS 21:10 ESV

Often the greatest hindrance to the best is the good. The greatest hindrance to Isaac is Ishmael.

There are many good things we can create, many good things we can do. But only one thing is needed (Luke 10:42). We have to discover the "one thing," and we only discover it when we are seated at the feet of Jesus. When we are only motivated by what JESUS needs, not what MAN needs and not what we think WE need, then we are on the path of continual and perpetual blessing.

September 17

"His mother said to the servants,
'Whatever He says to you, do it.'"
JOHN 2:5

If only we would heed this advice from Mary. To be sure she has learned this in years gone by. Through many experiences she has at last learned where to go. Her automatic reflex now is to go to Jesus and lay the problem at His feet: "They have no wine." That is all. In this relationship she makes no demands, she does not even ask Him outright to do something. He knows what she means. It is an understanding that is borne out of relationship.

This, brothers and sisters, is the whole purpose for the trial you find yourself in. It may be that you have no oil, no bread, no fish, or no wine. Whatever the situation, bring your problem to the Lord of Infinite Supply, and do whatever He says to do. He wishes to reveal His glory in you. He longs to see His Power displayed through your weakness. The very thing you see as a problem is really an opportunity to see Jesus in a depth you cannot otherwise see.

September 18

"In the world you will have tribulation; but be of
good cheer, I have overcome the world."
JOHN 16:33

Since we cannot avoid having tribulation in this world, we might as well make the best possible use of every circumstance we find ourselves in.

Begin to see all your temptations, tests, and trials as opportunities for growing, maturing, and learning how to live as an Overcomer. Then your problem will become your greatest opportunity for knowing God – for the depth of your revelation is measured by the depth of your suffering.

September 19

"Abide in Me, and I in you.
As the branch cannot bear fruit of itself,
unless it abides in the vine, neither can you,
unless you abide in Me."
JOHN 15:4

It is never a question of how to get the Life to flow, or how to get the Lord to move. To tap into the Infinite Supply it is only a matter of being yielded to the Lord and emptied of ourselves. When this happens then the Life will flow of its own accord.

On the negative side, this Life answers to every assault of the Adversary and stops his harassment against us. On the positive side, this Life supplies us with all the spiritual resources we need to maintain our abiding relationship with the Lord Jesus. With less of me, there will be more of the Lord: this is a spiritual law. Therefore, "He must increase, but I must decrease" (John 3:30).

September 20

"We rejoice in Christ Jesus, and have
no confidence in the flesh."
PHILIPPIANS 3:3

C an you see that "Self-Esteem" actually takes you further away from Christ-Esteem? Self-esteem increases Self. But Paul said we rejoice in Christ Jesus and have no confidence in the flesh. When I have lost confidence in myself then I can put all my confidence in Christ. He is increased as I am decreased.

Some years ago I was teaching at a men's retreat. I was met at the airport and we stopped to get something to eat on the way to the retreat area. The brothers were excited and looking forward to the weekend. One of them exclaimed, "I just want more of the Lord! More of the Lord!" I was about to agree when the Holy Spirit gave me a flash of new understanding. I said, "Brother, it is not more of the Lord that we need; we just need less of everything else!" Of course there is nothing wrong with wanting more of the Lord, but there is so much that gets in the way of Him already.

September 21

"You did not choose Me, but
I chose you and appointed you that you
should go and bear fruit, and that
your fruit should remain."
JOHN 15:16

W hen we allow the Holy Spirit to increase Christ, and when we allow the Cross to do its work of decreasing Self, the fruit will come forth in abundance. This makes everything we experience worthwhile. What is the fruit of the Spirit? It is the reward, the prize, the end result of all those seasons of increasing and decreasing: the character and nature of Christ reproduced in a person. It is the precious Seed finally coming into maturity.

The fruit of the Spirit is love, joy, peace, longsuffering, gentleness, goodness, faith, meekness, self-control. Against such there is no law (Galatians 5:22,23). Fruit is not how much work we can accomplish or how many things we can do for God. Fruit is, "How much of Christ can be seen in me instead of me?" The fruit of the Spirit is found in the transformed character of someone who walks with Jesus in the Difficult Path.

September 22

"He who overcomes, and keeps
My works until the end, to him I will give
power over the nations."
REVELATION 2:26

The Remnant is not an exclusive, elitist circle of super-spiritual saints. Not at all. The promises are made to the "whosoevers."

Anyone can be a friend of God! Anyone can overcome! But we know that everyone will not. Why won't they? I wish I knew why, I wish I could explain it, but I cannot explain it, and I just know it is a fact that everyone will not go on with God. We know it from history, we know it from looking around us right now. Everyone is not going to press into God, everyone is not going to seek His Kingdom, everyone is not going to lay down their life and follow Jesus. Not that they CANNOT, but they WILL NOT.

Anyone can, everyone won't (in fact, a large majority will not), but SOMEBODY will. That group of "somebodies" who will is the Remnant.

September 23

> "You are our Father; we are
> the clay, and You are our potter."
> ISAIAH 64:8 ESV

I went to a pottery once and watched the potter form a lump of clay into a jar. He demonstrated the technique and in his skilled hands the jar began to take shape. But there was something about it that was not quite right, something was a little off. I didn't see anything wrong with it, but the potter did. So he just crushed the whole thing back into a shapeless lump like it was no big deal and started again.

Notice that he did not throw the lump away and say the lump was no good. Nor did he blame the lump for not turning out correctly. Nor did he get angry, frustrated, or upset. It was just easier for him to start over with the lump and work with it until it was perfect.

Well, that was encouraging to me! The lump really couldn't do anything to help itself get any better, or make itself more worthy. It was just a lump, yielded to the potter's hands.

September 24

"It is no longer I who live, but
Christ who lives in me."
GALATIANS 2:20

Most of us are still trying to attain something and have not yet realized that we have already obtained it. We wear ourselves out in order to be Christ-like. We are hoping that through much effort we will one day reach some standard to which we can finally say we are living like Jesus. But this is not God's way.

It is not a changed life that God seeks from you, but an exchanged life – that is, your life is to be given up in exchange for His Life. That is the exchanged Life: my life for His Life.

September 25

"You younger people, submit yourselves to
your elders. Yes, all of you be submissive to one
another, and be clothed with humility."
1 PETER 5:5

I f our desire is for maturity, that is, if we desire to come to the full-knowledge of Christ and grow up into Him in all things, we should naturally pay attention to those who are elder in the Lord. My elder brother, or my elder sister, has walked with the Lord longer than I have. The implication is that they are more conformed to the image of Christ than myself; they have experienced a deeper work of the Cross than I have; thus, they have more practical wisdom than I do, they have something to teach me, and I need to hear Christ in them so I, too, can grow.

It should be obvious to you who is, and who is not, your elder in the Lord. And, it should be plain to see that not everyone who is older is necessarily elder. If you say you are a believer but you live no differently from the world, then you can be as old as Methuselah yet you are certainly not an elder.

September 26

"Blessed are the peacemakers, for they
shall be called sons of God."
MATTHEW 5:9

Peacemakers are simply agents of Grace, showing people the way to the Prince of Peace. Peacemakers are ambassadors sent to represent the King and His Kingdom.

What is the message? It is the message of reconciliation, the message that all is forgiven, the message of hope, and love, and grace, and a thousand other good things (see 2 Corinthians 5:17-21). It is the most awe-inspiring mission a human being could ever have: to represent Heaven in the midst of Hell; Light in the midst of Darkness; Liberty in the midst of Bondage; to proclaim the preeminence and Lordship of Jesus when we do not yet see all things submitted to Him (Hebrews 2:8). And to do all this in a way that does not drive people away or turn them off, but causes them to fall in love with Him and make their peace with Him – not through forced submission, manipulation, or fear – but willingly, gladly.

September 27

"I therefore, a prisoner for the Lord, urge you..."
EPHESIANS 4:1 ESV

To be the prisoner of the Lord means that we accept the sentence of death and are resigned to our fate. We are not the Lord's prisoner if we are still protesting our innocence. If we do not agree with the Lord that Self is worthy of death then we unnecessarily delay the inevitable.

If we must take up the Cross and be crucified, it is better to submit ourselves to it as Christ did, giving up our spirit into the Father's hands, and bowing our head in peace. So let us drink the Cup that the Father gives us. If we struggle and protest, like the two thieves, then we only prolong our agony, and the soldiers must come and break our legs. Either way, the Cross means death. The sooner we surrender to it, the sooner we find Resurrection.

September 28

"When you do a charitable deed, do not let your
left hand know what your right hand is doing."
MATTHEW 6:3

J esus did not advocate anonymous charity in order to make us paranoid or fearful of being caught doing a good deed. He did it to liberate us, to enlarge us, to help us experience the pure joy of a no-strings-attached gift, to ensure we would not become proud, and very importantly, to prevent others from rewarding, manipulating, regulating, or expecting us to give to them on a continual basis apart from His direction.

He understood how easily people, even with the best of intentions, make value judgments of others based on material possessions. He obviously didn't want that to be the case among His people.

September 29

*"He who establishes us with you
in Christ and has anointed us is God."*
2 CORINTHIANS 1:21

I f we have Him then we have everything that is in Him already. If only we can get less of everything else, there will be more of Him revealed! With less of me there will be more of Him.

Jesus said that "only One Thing is needed," but like Martha, we have become troubled over "many things" (Luke 10:40-42). When those many things are discarded, and we are decreased, then we are free to focus our attention on the One Thing that really matters, and Christ is increased in us. This is why we say that spiritual growth is not more knowledge or increase of years; it is simply more of Him and less of me. He increases as I am decreased. This is what it means to be a disciple. This is how Christ becomes preeminent over us individually. It does not happen all at once, but over the process of many temptations, tests, trials, and a fair amount of suffering. I call it being reduced to Christ.

September 30

"Oh the depth of the riches
both of the wisdom and knowledge of God!
How unsearchable are His judgments, and
His ways past finding out!"
ROMANS 11:33

To illustrate, let us imagine that we here on earth desire to reach the moon. That is a definitive goal which we can see. We can measure the distance and make plans to reach the moon. To us here on earth that is the ultimate in space exploration. Now let us imagine that one day we reach the moon. Just as we become acclimated to this enormous triumph, our eyes turn upward yet again and we see the vast expanse of space, the innumerable stars, planets, and galaxies, stretched out before us for more than 15,000,000,000 light years, and enlarging its borders faster than we could ever hope to keep up. We will never get to the end of it.

This, in a nutshell, is what it is to find ourselves lost in the depths of Christ. The more we know of Him, the less we realize we know.

October 1

"That I may know Him and the power
of His resurrection, and the fellowship of His
sufferings, being conformed to His death, if, by
any means, I may attain to the resurrection from
the dead. Not that I have already attained, or am
already perfected; but I press on, that I may lay
hold of that for which Christ Jesus has
also laid hold of me."
PHILIPPIANS 3:10-12

M any years after having first put on the Lord Jesus, Paul declares that he is still trying to apprehend the One Who has already apprehended him. The height, width, breadth, length, and depth of this New Man, this Heavenly Man, is quite beyond what we can measure apart from Spirit-revelation. We are more familiar with and have more confidence in the old man than we do in the New Man. By the grace of God, this has to change. When we truly see the New Man we transcend the old man. And this, in a nutshell, is how God accomplishes the work of decreasing us and increasing Christ.

October 2

"I am the Lord, I do not change."
MALACHI 3:6

God sees all things before they happen, therefore God is never surprised or disappointed. Since He is never disappointed, He can never be discouraged. Since He is never discouraged, we can be confident that He will accomplish, perfect, and complete what He sets out to do no matter how far off course or dark things seem to get.

His Will and His Kingdom are not optional. His Will is not a mere wish or a hope. His Word is a statement of purpose, a foregone conclusion. Since God created time, He is above, beyond, and outside of time; therefore, the passage of time does not diminish His Will one iota. He is as zealous for the accomplishment and fulfillment of His Will today as He was 2,000 years ago, and at creation. He does not tire, He does not become stressed out, He does not become unenthusiastic. We can always rely upon the zealous, persistent Purpose of God.

October 3

"Jews request a sign, and Greeks seek after
wisdom; but we preach Christ crucified."
1 CORINTHIANS 1:22,23

Unfortunately, salvation as preached today results not in death, but in "swooning." There is an ecstatic joy and the "near death experience" of a token surrender, but it is not real death. The convert merely changes his conduct, cries a few tears, yet he still lives. The outward deportment may be different, but he has not died. He commences to follow the Lord and fill his life with spiritual activity, but his many failures and shortcomings prove something is missing in his experience. What is it?

He knows the Cross only as something Jesus died on for him. The Cross does not represent his own death, but his Lord's death. It is seldom presented as anything other than the means of atonement and forgiveness of sins. Few realize it is the means by which we enter, as well as live, the Christian life.

October 4

"In my prosperity I said,
'I shall never be moved.'"
PSALM 30:6

I t should be obvious that God will not give us grace while we are still proud. Why? Because He will allow no flesh to glory in His presence. When we cease doing what we cannot do then He begins to do what we cannot. The problem is that we still think we can do so many things. We must learn sooner, rather than later, that "apart from Me you can do nothing" (John 15:5). *Nothing!*

But it is human nature to try and do it ourselves. This human nature is the flesh. It prevents us from entering into Grace. God cannot save someone who is still trying to save themselves. Similarly, God cannot do what we are still trying to do. He will wait – weeks, months, or years – until we have exhausted our strength. When our strength is completely gone and we finally go to Him in weakness, He becomes our Strength and we find Grace is there to do the impossible. Then we know it was not us, but the Lord. All praise goes to Him, and we retain nothing for ourselves.

October 5

"She had a sister called Mary, who also sat at
Jesus' feet and heard His word."
LUKE 10:39

There are two elements here: she sat at His feet, and she heard His Word. You must sit at His feet and hear Him for yourself. Entering into the Lord's thought, becoming acquainted with His Ways as well as His Word, takes the sort of love-devotion Mary demonstrates.

The Greek here is continuous action: she "kept on listening." Martha listened too, but when she arose to prepare dinner, Mary remained. As we progress we will see that Mary has discovered Spirit and Truth, and from henceforth she is always at the feet of the Lord in one way or the other.

October 6

"As for the one who is weak in faith, welcome
him, but not to quarrel over opinions."
ROMANS 14:1 ESV

My children are immature, but I cannot expect them to be anything other than immature so long as they are children. I am lovingly committed to their long-term growth. In the same way, let us not despise the spiritually immature or the weak in faith. Instead, the Word tells us to receive them and watch over them. For those of you who are further along, never forget how many years of God's dealings it took to bring you to the level of experience you take for granted today.

October 7

"By this we know love, because
He laid down His life for us. And we also ought to
lay down our lives for the brethren."
1 JOHN 3:16

This increase of Christ and decrease of Self does not begin on a universal level, but goes to work individually, quietly, in the innermost being of every true disciple. This process of increasing Christ and decreasing Self began long before you even gave your heart to the Lord. It made the actual giving of your heart to Him possible. But He must continue to increase, and so this process of increase will continue beyond that initial coming to the Lord and will be the means through which you are to grow spiritually.

In like manner, you must continue to decrease, and so that process of decrease will continue beyond that initial coming to the Lord and will also be the means through which you are to grow spiritually. You need both the increase and the decrease. They both work together, and one is not possible without the other.

October 8

"And [God] raised us up
together, and made us sit together in
the heavenly places in Christ Jesus."
EPHESIANS 2:6

D o you see yourself seated with Christ in the heavenlies? Paul saw it, and prayed the Ephesians would see it. When the Lord showed me that I was raised together with Christ and was made to sit (past tense) in the heavenly places with Christ, do you think it changed the way I saw the world? Absolutely! No more was I looking at things from "ground level," but from the heavenly realm.

Things look decidedly different when viewed from above.

October 9

"'You have put all things in
subjection under His feet.' For in that He put
all in subjection under Him, He left nothing
that is not put under Him."
HEBREWS 2:8

T his possession and subjection of all things to Christ is not a passive, disinterested, distant, absentee ownership, like a clock that was once wound and now ticks all by itself long after the watchmaker has left it. Make no mistake: at the core of this spiritual and physical universe is a living, powerful, proactive Personality at work to bring fallen creation back to its original state, back into line with God's Purpose, Heart, Mind, Desire, and Plan, which is CHRIST FILLING ALL THINGS, CHRIST UPHOLDING ALL THINGS, CHRIST AT THE CENTER OF ALL THINGS!

Come quickly Lord Jesus! May Your Kingdom be manifest!

October 10

"Who am I, that I should go to
Pharaoh, and that I should bring forth the
children of Israel out of Egypt? O my Lord,
I am not eloquent... but I am slow of
speech, and slow of tongue."
EXODUS 3:11; 4:10

We know that in fact Moses was mighty in words and in deeds (Acts 7:22). But he no longer saw that as an asset anymore.

That is exactly the type of person that God is looking for. He is not searching for those naturally gifted souls who think they can do it and then set out in their own strength! It is those who embrace the weakness of the Cross and allow God's strength to be perfected in them that He is looking for.

October 11

"When they saw the boldness of
Peter and John, and perceived that they
were uneducated and untrained men,
they marveled. And they realized that
they had been with Jesus."
ACTS 4:13

When people are in your presence, what do they touch – a system of beliefs, a code of conduct, an ethical standard, or a Person? We may have an abundance of words and teachings, but all of them together are nothing but letters if they are not constantly pointing us to a Living Christ.

October 12

"Master, we have toiled all night and
caught nothing; nevertheless at Your word
I will let down the net."
LUKE 5:5

When we cease trying to do what we cannot do then the Lord will begin to do what only He can do anyway. "And when they had done [what Jesus said to do] they caught a great number of fish, and their net was breaking" (Luke 5:6). Peter, James, and John can try as they might and do their best, but without the word of the Lord it is in vain. They might have saved themselves a lot of effort had they sought the word of the Lord to begin with.

Which would you rather have: a whole night of wasted effort on your own, or five minutes of abundance with the Lord? Yes we should work, but first we must wait. And if we will wait for the Lord then we will have Infinite Supply for the work at hand.

October 13

"In Him... being predestined according
to the purpose of Him who works all things
according to the counsel of His will."
EPHESIANS 1:11

Here we have a three-fold witness to God's Ultimate Purpose and Intention in Christ. First, God has a Will. Second, God's Will is "all things in Christ." Third, God is working all things according to this Purpose.

The fact that God has a Will, and works everything according to this Will, is critical. There is a Purpose, a reason for being. Nothing is created apart from this Purpose. You are not an accident; you are not a mistake; you are not just a quirk of fate or a victim of circumstance. There is no such thing as "luck." There is an infinitely wise Creator Who stands behind His Creation, and He has brought nothing into being without having first completed it in His Own Mind first. He does not make things up as He goes along, reacting to difficulties with a new contingency plan when things do not go as expected. God has no "Plan B." He uses everything – the good, the bad, and the ugly – to accomplish His Purpose.

October 14

"Be faithful until death, and I will give
you the crown of life... He who overcomes shall
not be hurt by the second death."
REVELATION 2:10,11

T he Crown of Life comes to those who lose
their life daily in order to gain His Life
daily. Overcomers cannot be hurt by death
because they have already died – not once, but
thousands of times: taking up the Cross daily,
denying Self, and following the Lord. Thus, the
highest call is not to lay down our physical life
as a martyr, but to lay down our Self life as a
disciple.

We can lay down our physical life in an
instant, but to take up the Cross daily is the
truest test, and much more difficult. It requires
us to be "faithful unto death." This is the secret
of the Overcomers.

October 15

"We also eagerly wait for the Savior,
the Lord Jesus Christ... He is able even to
subdue all things to Himself."
PHILIPPIANS 3:20,21

Everything is moving back TOWARDS a Christocentric universe, so that as it was in the beginning, so it will be in the ending. Just as all things have their source and beginning in Christ, so all things will have their ending in Christ. He subdues all things, in order to gather together and reconcile all things, that He may fill all things.

What a task that is! How can that be? How can all things ever be subdued, gathered together into one, reconciled, and filled by Christ? We cannot say how, but we know that "He is able." Praise God, how can we doubt Him? How can we question this Man? Do we not yet know that He is the Preeminent One? Let us bow down and thank and praise God that He is able!

October 16

"Jesus lifted up His eyes, and seeing
a great multitude coming toward Him, He said to
Philip, 'Where shall we buy bread, that these may
eat?' But this He said to test him, for He
Himself knew what He would do."
JOHN 6:5,6

When we see a need we grow frustrated. But when Jesus sees a need He already knows what He wants to do. Not only will He meet the need, but He will reveal Himself in the process. Sometimes He will leave the need unmet, at least for a season, and just reveal Himself to us as All that we need (2 Corinthians 12:8,9).

This explains why it sometimes appears that the Lord delays in answering us. He already knows what He is going to do, but we do not know. He waits for us to see if we will trust Him as Infinite Supply. Is Jesus "Lord" only after He answers us? Or is Jesus "Lord" whether He answers us or not? The Lord's "proving ground" is just there, in between the Need and the Answer. And sometimes it is, indeed, quite a stretching, and a thorough test.

October 17

"We do not yet see all things put
under Him; but we see Jesus."
HEBREWS 2:8,9

Today, Scripture acknowledges, we do not YET see all things submitted to Him. I must say I find that word "YET" terribly exciting! That word "YET" means that something is in store for everything that remains unsubmitted to the Lord Jesus Christ. The presence of the word "YET" means its manifestation is inevitable.

We are not pretending to see something that does not really exist – yes, we agree that we do not YET see all things submitted to Him, things are bad, and will probably get worse; BUT we do see JESUS, and for the Christian who seeks first the Kingdom of God, that revelation is sufficient. You may see every fact to the contrary and argue against Him, but we see Who He is by revelation, and by revelation we know that what we see happening in the unsubmitted earth today will be set in order when Christ and His Kingdom are manifest in all of creation.

October 18

"All authority has been given to Me
in heaven and on earth."
MATTHEW 28:18

The only legitimate power in the universe belongs to the Lord Jesus – all other power is either illegitimate or temporal. If THE power belongs to Him, then it cannot belong to anyone else. Jesus says, "All authority [power] has been given to Me in heaven and on earth." That is a very broad statement, is it not? Absolute power over all of creation!

In a world in which men (and devils) wrestle for dominion, joust for position, seek the preeminence for themselves, strive to exert their influence over others, and lust for more and more control over one another, we as the Body of Christ may simply raise our hands to heaven and lift up our eyes to our Head in Whom God has vested all of His omnipotence and declare to the universe, "YOURS IS THE POWER, and apart from You, we can do nothing."

October 19

"You meant evil against me;
but God meant it for good."
GENESIS 50:20

The story of Joseph is not just the story of Joseph. It is the story of how God works everything together for His Purpose. No matter how far removed from that Purpose things seem to get, eventually we see its fulfillment.

At some point in eternity we will all stand before God and will finally see His Ultimate Purpose fulfilled. Then we will look back on the sad history of the human race and we will see how God brought something good out of every evil thing that ever rose up to challenge His Purpose. For some people the existence of evil is a stumbling block. If God is good, why does He allow evil? A better question is: how can God allow evil and still manage to bring something good out of it in the end? Evil is not a stumbling block to an all-powerful, all-knowing Creator who specializes in bringing good out of evil. What He did for Joseph He will do for all Creation.

October 20

"We know that the whole creation groans and labors with birth pangs together until now."
ROMANS 8:22

J ust as all things are working together towards God's purpose of increasing Christ, so all things are working together towards decreasing us. It does not matter if we understand it or comprehend it. It does not matter if you believe in it or agree with it. You are being decreased just the same, and Christ is being increased. It MUST be so, therefore it IS so.

Scientists call this decreasing "entropy," and it means, "inevitable and steady deterioration." We can observe this in creation. The present things are groaning and laboring in pain, deteriorating in order to make way for a new heaven and a new earth. We begin to die as soon as we are born. We can look in our own bodies for evidence of "inevitable and steady deterioration" as we move towards a redeemed body. But more importantly, WE, the "I," the "Self," is being decreased that Christ may fill us.

October 21

"To him who overcomes I will
give to eat from the tree of life, which is in
the midst of the Paradise of God."
REVELATION 2:7

We should see that Christ does more than restore what Adam lost. He goes beyond Adam, offering the Overcomers fruit from the Tree of Life, fruit Adam knows nothing about. Obviously this is symbolic language, but what does it mean? The Tree of Life represents the Cross, for from that Tree the Lord yielded up His Life for us all. Those who overcome have learned that fruitfulness and Life come from death to Self, and that is what the Cross means. The Cross is a Tree of Life to those who embrace it.

October 22

"In Him we live and move
and have our being."
ACTS 17:28

The Law of Life means that I do not try to be or do anything in my own strength. Instead, the Life leads me, the Life instructs me, and the Life gives me the words and the actions.

I am not a Christian because I believe in the Bible, follow the teachings of Jesus, and live a good life. I am a Christian because Christ is my Life. Since Christ is my Life, I no longer live, but it is Christ Who lives in me. I do nothing to achieve this, it just is. Because He lives, I live.

October 23

"'Who do you say that I am?'
Simon Peter answered and said, 'You are the
Christ, the Son of the living God.'"
MATTHEW 16:15,16

J esus did not teach Peter what to say, He merely revealed Himself to Peter. He did not sit down with His disciples and say, "I am the Christ, the Son of the Living God. Now repeat that after Me several times, and I will test you on this in the morning." He did not teach them a catechism or a rosary or a mantra or a confession, He merely revealed Himself to them as He in fact is. They made the confession in due course, having revelation.

The Testimony of Jesus always springs forth from the Revelation of Christ. If we do not have the Revelation then we cannot have the Testimony. That is to say, we cannot bear witness of what we have seen and heard if we have not, in fact, seen or heard anything. We try to get people to confess in order that they may ATTAIN to something, but true confession comes forth naturally after they have OBTAINED it.

October 24

"He died for all, that those who live
should live no longer for themselves, but for Him
who died for them and rose again."
2 CORINTHIANS 5:15

With less of me, there will be more of Him in my life, so why would I resist that? There should be less of me today than there was yesterday, and there should be more of Him now than there was before. If I will submit to Him today, then tomorrow there will be yet a little more of Him and a little less of me. Praise God! Spiritual growth is not stronger anointing, greater power, or increased knowledge. Spiritual growth is "He must increase, but I must decrease" (John 3:30).

October 25

"'Most assuredly, I say to you,
Moses did not give you the bread from
heaven, but My Father gives you the true bread
from heaven. For the bread of God is He who
comes down from heaven and gives life to the
world.' Then they said to Him, 'Lord, give us
this bread always.' And Jesus said to
them, 'I am the bread of life.'"
JOHN 6:32-35

The people were asking for Jesus to give them bread, but failed to recognize that He Himself is the Bread of Life. They worked and toiled for something which would perish, but were not willing to receive the True Bread that would not perish.

The significance of the Lord Jesus is not that He can give us bread, but that He *is* the Bread.

October 26

"Paul, a prisoner of Christ Jesus..."
PHILEMON 1:1

It is a glorious thing to be the prisoner of the Lord, for in our bonds we find liberty. In our weakness we find strength. In our foolishness we find wisdom. In our poverty we find prosperity. By losing everything we find everything. By giving up all things we inherit all things. By accepting the sentence of death we find the Life of the Lord.

Let us stretch forth our hands and allow Him to dress us and lead us where He wishes us to go, in the way we would not choose for ourselves, for that is the Narrow Way, and it is the path of blessing, though it be disguised.

October 27

"God, who created all things
through Jesus Christ."
EPHESIANS 3:9

If you walk into a dark house and find the furniture scattered and the rooms covered with dust and spider webs everywhere, you would probably conclude that no one had lived there for some time. But if you walk into a house and find the lights are on, the rooms are tastefully decorated, the furniture is arranged in an orderly fashion, the table is set and dinner is cooking on the stove then you would not be surprised to find someone lives there and has put everything in its place.

The more we look at creation the easier it is to believe that there is Someone with infinite wisdom Who designed everything with purposeful intention according to a definite order and arrangement. The Scripture says that this Someone is God, Who "created all things through Jesus Christ."

October 28

"O My Father, if it is possible, let
this cup pass from Me; nevertheless, not
as I will, but as You will."
MATTHEW 26:39

H is sweat mingled with His tears, and He wrestled with Himself three times before He could settle the issue, but once it was settled, He gave no resistance, and within a few hours everything was accomplished.

Oh! That is where we are lacking today! How long will we kick and struggle against the pricks? How long will we argue and complain against God and resist His dealings with us? If we have to die in order to truly live, let us be about the business of dying! If we must be crucified in order to have Resurrection Life, then let us just submit to it and get it over with!

October 29

"Of that day and hour no one knows,
not even the angels in heaven, nor the Son, but
only the Father. Take heed, watch and pray; for
you do not know when the time is... And
what I say to you, I say to all: Watch!"
MARK 13:32,33,37

The Kingdom may be near, at hand, at the door, even within; but it has not come in its fullness until the King Himself returns. This is the sense in which Jesus calls upon us to watch and pray for the Kingdom to come. It is literally praying that the King will come into the fullness of His Kingdom – not merely within the heart of the individual believer, but in a tangible, visible, universal sense that brings about the full recovery of the Heavenly Order with Christ once more having the preeminence in all things.

October 30

"We had the sentence of death in
ourselves, that we should not trust in ourselves
but in God who raises the dead."
2 CORINTHIANS 1:9

Know that Christ is not here to help you become a better person, but to make you so weak in yourself and so sick of your own way that you can do nothing but trust in Him to do what you at last realize you cannot do. It does not matter if that something "we cannot do" is save ourselves, control our temper, get along with others, raise our children, or overcome a lustful habit. The course is the same. After many attempts and failures we at last realize we cannot, so we throw ourselves on the mercy of God and trust Him to do what we cannot do.

October 31

> "The Lord is near to those who have a
> broken heart, and saves such as have a contrite
> spirit. Many are the afflictions of the righteous,
> but the Lord delivers him out of them all."
> PSALM 34:18,19

We must learn sooner rather than later that discipleship is a process of tearing down in order to build up. We cannot expect to have a single mountaintop experience with the Lord and then assume from henceforth the work of the Cross is completed in us. When we are standing with the Lord in the New Jerusalem we may lay down the Cross. Until then, we dare not entertain the thought that we have already been made perfect. We must deny ourselves and take up the Cross daily.

November 1

"Yours is the Kingdom, and the Power,
and the Glory forever. Amen."
MATTHEW 6:13

There is a Remnant of called-out ones who have seen the Glory of the Son and WILL seek the interests of God's Only Begotten One. In a time when men solicit the glory and honor and power from one another, there is a Holy Nation of priests and kings who will give the Son the glory He deserves, declaring, "YOURS IS THE GLORY, we will render to You, and to You alone, the glory due Your Name."

November 2

"Bring out the best robe and put it on him."
LUKE 15:22

To put on the Lord Jesus is to be clothed with the very best robe. This robe makes us look better than we really are. But when we are dressed with the best we begin to act differently. Having put on the Lord Jesus, we are clothed with Him and His character replaces our character. His Life is received in exchange for our life. If we cooperate with the Life we will naturally find our behavior is changed.

But what of the elder son? "Son, you are always with me, and all that I have is yours" (Luke 15:31). Hallelujah! There is no partiality with God, however much we may think God is being more fair or more generous to some brother or sister. Not so: the robe, the ring, and the shoes only represent the "all," the fullness of the Father, and "of His fullness we have all received" (John 1:16). The Father says, "All that I have is yours!" Who can dare ask God for a single thing apart from the Son?

November 3

"Without Me you can do nothing."
JOHN 15:5

Jesus would explain to His disciples that spiritual life hinges upon living in active dependence upon Himself. That is the fundamental lesson to learn because it is the fundamental sin of mankind – the independent path. Jesus says without Him we can do nothing. Nothing! But it is human nature to try and do something in ourselves. We call it freedom and liberty; blazing our own trail; making something happen. But the end result is death and destruction.

The fall of man illustrates a fundamental truth: that whenever Self is allowed to rule in the place of Christ, the result is sin, sorrow, separation and death. Apart from Him we really can do nothing.

November 4

"To him who overcomes I will give
to eat from the tree of life."
REVELATION 2:7

L ike Adam, we can choose to eat from either tree, but we cannot eat from both. Adam sinned when he fell into the flesh and yielded to his Self-life. He rejected the Tree of Life in favor of something that was "good... pleasant... and desirable" (Genesis 3:6). The Cross does not look like a Tree of Life at all. It is neither good, nor pleasant, nor desirable. It looks like death. Perhaps this is why Adam did not eat from it first. But God's End is not death, regardless of appearances: God's End is Life out of death, which is resurrection. To eat of the fruit of the Tree of Life is to glory in the Cross of Jesus Christ and find Life out of death. It is becoming popular to preach and teach about the Cross these days, but how many are eating of its fruit? Can we really see the Cross as the TREE OF LIFE, and are we eating its fruit? We will know a true disciple of the Lord, not by words, but by fruit, and the Cross is the Tree of Life from which this fruit comes.

November 5

"No one can serve two masters,
for either he will hate the one and love the
other, or he will be devoted to the one
and despise the other."
MATTHEW 6:24

The context of this passage is talking about mammon (the love of, and the endless pursuit of, wealth). But the principle applies to everything else. There can only be one master in your life. You can only serve one thing at a time. You are not free to do as you please. Even if you say you serve no one, you are still serving Self. So which will it be? Jesus says if you love Him then you will hate everything else. What does that mean?

It means that you will allow nothing and no one to take the place of the One you love – not for a day, not for an hour, not for a minute. If our love for the Lord is strong then we will learn to hate everything which competes against Him. We will despise anything that seeks to hinder our relationship with Christ.

November 6

"He, the Spirit of truth...
will guide you into all truth."
JOHN 16:13

To choose the Truth is to want the Truth at all costs, even if it means sacrificing everything I have believed up until now, challenging all my paradigms, questioning all my teachers, examining everything I have ever experienced.

Of course our first decision about Truth is based upon Who Jesus is. With that question settled many Christians are content, but Truth is living. Truth will continue to reveal Himself to us and around us for as long as we will allow it. What, after all, is Wisdom? Wisdom is the ability to see things from heaven's, and thus God's, perspective. Daily we must choose between ignorant bliss or seeing things as God sees them. It is a daily choice. You cannot be told, you have to see it for yourself.

November 7

"I know Whom I have believed."
2 TIMOTHY 1:12

A certain brother was always emphatic about what he believed until someone with equal or greater argument confronted him. This occurred one day when someone pointed out several supposed "errors" in the Bible. This caused the brother to be very alarmed. He went to an elderly sister and informed her of these alleged errors and wanted to know her opinion. She simply stated that the knowledge of God did not depend upon the answering of these questions.

He thought, perhaps not to you, but to me it is important! So he spent the next year investigating what this other person had told him and found it to be untrue. But, had he simply known God He would not have found it necessary to study the whole thing and reason it out. The elderly sister was right, the knowledge of God did not depend upon the answering of those questions. If you know Who, knowing what and why become less significant.

November 8

"We have left all and followed You."
MARK 10:28

Here is a golden truth: if He possesses all that YOU have, then you will possess all that HE has. Allow that truth to sink into your heart. Breathe it in and out. Let the Holy Spirit soak it into the pores of your soul and you will not be able to contain His joy and peace emanating from you. You will start giving things up that before you would have never let go. You will gladly relinquish everything.

November 9

"He appointed twelve,
that they might be with Him..."
MARK 3:14

The first order of business was not the preaching or the sending forth; it was simply being with Jesus. During those times of being alone and apart with Christ He revealed Himself to them in a deep way. They walked with Him, watched Him, and listened to Him for three and a half years. Just as importantly, they learned to walk with each other. They learned how to serve one another in love. When Jesus finally did send them forth to preach they actually had something worth sharing and worth listening to.

Your primary calling as a disciple is to BE with Jesus, because that is how you LEARN OF HIM. It is not learning about the Christian faith – that is a thing. It is not learning about Bible doctrine – that is a thing. It is not learning about Christian things or religious things or spiritual things. It is not learning about the Bible. It's not even learning ABOUT Jesus, it is learning OF Jesus FROM Jesus.

November 10

"God resists the proud."
JAMES 4:6

Our automatic assumption is that anything which resists us or hinders us is of satanic origin. Yet we learn from James 4:6 that there is Someone Else who can resist us. There is Another Who carefully watches what we do, and frequently hinders us from making progress. It comes as a shock and surprise to some Christians to see one day that God, not the devil, is resisting them. The Lord Himself resists us, closes doors, causes things to be unfruitful, and spoils all our plans. How so? Because "God resists the proud."

This resistance from God is insurmountable. It is a fearful thing to fight the Lord. We spend most of our lives wrestling with God instead of cooperating with God, and in the end we have nothing to show for it. So much time and effort is wasted because we proceed in our own, stubborn way. We attribute all difficulties to the devil, or to other people, or our circumstances, or our environment, and fail to recognize that the Lord Himself is resisting us.

November 11

"To him who overcomes I will give
some of the hidden manna to eat. And I will
give him a white stone, and on the stone a new
name written which no one knows
except him who receives it."
REVELATION 2:17

The manna is HIDDEN and the name is SECRET. The Lord is doing a work, but that work is, for the most part, hidden and secret. If we are always looking for something out in the open and in plain view then we will miss the deeper workings of God below the surface.

November 12

"Who is he who overcomes the world, but he
who believes that Jesus is the Son of God?"
1 JOHN 5:5

The Lord's answer to a state of decline is to reveal Himself and His eternal purpose. Once the Lord has established for Himself a people that will represent His interests, then He will move immediately to secure, protect, establish, and strengthen the Remnant. Here is what I want us to see. When we align ourselves with God's Thought, with God's Kingdom, and with God's Will in Christ, we are invincible.

November 13

"I press toward the goal for the prize of the
upward call of God in Christ Jesus."
PHILIPPIANS 3:14

G od has a purpose for the universe: that in all things Christ would have the pre-eminence. This is the Heavenly Bullseye. Since you, dear reader, are part of the universe, you are one of those "all things." So this purpose includes you.

Actually, this is the same purpose He had in mind for Adam: that Christ would have the preeminence in him. But Adam chose an independent path and failed to give Christ the preeminence. He took the preeminence for himself. Adam missed the mark, which is a life submitted to, and totally dependent upon, God.

November 14

"The Most High rules
in the kingdoms of men."
DANIEL 4:17

C hrist is increasing and filling all things.
Have you seen this? If you have, then
embrace it, submit to it, cooperate with it, be in
harmony with it, order your life around it,
demonstrate it to the world around you, and
pray for its fulfillment.

Get aligned with something and Someone
higher and greater than yourself. For when you
see God's Purpose, and you adjust your life
according to that Purpose, and you consistently
pray for the fulfillment of that Purpose, then
His Purpose cannot be stopped; His Will
cannot be frustrated; His Kingdom cannot be
defeated. Heaven singles you out and Hell
trembles with fear. You just became
undefeatable! You just joined the Remnant.

November 15

"Teacher, this woman was
caught in adultery, in the very act. Now Moses,
in the law, commanded us that such should be
stoned. But what do You say?"
JOHN 8:4,5

Legally they were on solid ground. But to her accusers, Jesus replied, "He who is without sin among you, let him throw a stone at her first." And when they all left, being convicted by their own conscience, He said to the woman: "Neither do I condemn you. Go, and sin no more" (John 8:12). We must conclude that however good the Law was, it did not represent God's highest, or God's best.

Jesus represents the holiness and purity of the Law but emphasized the part that had been too long overlooked: grace and humility. He came to address the deeper issues of the heart, and in so doing, showed us what God really intended from the beginning. He did not destroy the Law, He superseded the Law! Thus He fulfilled the spirit of the Law – even if it sometimes appeared as if He did not follow the letter of the Law.

November 16

"When it pleased God... to reveal
His Son in me... I did not immediately confer with
flesh and blood, nor did I go up to Jerusalem to
those who were apostles before me."
GALATIANS 1:15-17

P aul did not seek credentials, ordination, or affiliation with a human organization. He did not wait for anyone to confirm the call on his life. He did not seek for hands to be laid on him. Preaching the gospel of Jesus Christ was renegade enough, but to preach the gospel to the Gentiles was a departure from the norm for the Christians at that time. It would later prove to be quite controversial and divisive. Prudence would dictate that it would be better to check with the other apostles and get their opinion and feedback before striking out in a new direction. Yet, Paul says once he obtained revelation he had no need to confer with flesh and blood.

Why? Because he was a maverick, an independent spirit, a rebel? No, it is only because the Revelation of Jesus is sufficient guidance. Flesh and blood cannot add to or take away from the Revelation.

November 17

*"I determined not to know anything among you
except Jesus Christ and Him crucified."*
1 CORINTHIANS 2:2

We can quote these teachings of Jesus, seek to imitate Him as our Example, strive to walk the narrow Way, and even accomplish many good deeds in His Name. But apart from the Cross these activities are wood, hay and stubble.

In calling us to come back to the Cross, God is asking us to lay down our lives and embrace the Wisdom of death, burial, resurrection, and ascension in order to live as sons and daughters within the Kingdom of God. Apart from the Cross we can neither enter the Kingdom nor live in the Spirit, no matter how great the desire. For apart from the Cross, we do not know what it is to turn the other cheek, to go the extra mile, to love our enemies, to pray for those who persecute us. Apart from the Cross, we do not know what it is to submit to the will of God, accept suffering, and cast ourselves upon Him. Apart from the Cross, we do not know what Resurrection is.

November 18

"Till we all come to the unity of the faith
and of the knowledge of the Son of God, to a
perfect man, to the measure of the stature
of the fullness of Christ."
EPHESIANS 4:13

I t is the FULLNESS of Christ that we are after, the revelation of Christ as He IN FACT IS. For too many Christians the Lord Jesus is "merely" their Savior. Thank God He is our Savior, but there is a depth and a richness bound up into the personage of Christ that goes far, far beyond "mere" salvation. Salvation is the narrow gate – coming into the fullness of Christ is the narrow path. The gate is only the entrance to something larger.

November 19

"All of you be submissive to
one another, and be clothed with humility,
for 'God resists the proud, but gives
grace to the humble.'"
1 PETER 5:5

The single requirement for grace is humility. But what is grace? Grace is more than just a theological term used to describe how we are saved. Grace is the power of God at work in my life to do what cannot be done in my own strength. Grace is energizing and proactive. When I have reached the end of myself then Grace Himself takes over and does what I am unable to do. In the first place, what I cannot do is save myself, and so I trust in the Grace of God, Jesus Christ, to save me.

But Grace will not only bring me through the Gate; He will bring me down the Path. Grace does not just get me started in the right direction, but goes along with me every step of the way. For Grace is a Man!

November 20

"It is not for you to know times or seasons that
the Father has fixed by His own authority."
Acts 1:7 ESV

They had asked, "Lord, will You at this time restore the Kingdom to Israel?" The response from Jesus is anticlimactic to the impatient. The King will not be forced, or rushed, or pushed into action. Jesus said, "It is not for you to know the times and the seasons."

The Kingdom of God is progressive – growing up from a single seed into an abundant tree with many branches and much fruit. Those seedlings were just freshly planted in eleven men and they would not come to maturity all at once but over the course of many seasons of increase and decrease. We cannot speculate as to when He will return in the power and glory of His Kingdom. We must "watch therefore, for you know neither the day nor the hour in which the Son of Man is coming."

November 21

"I die daily."
1 CORINTHIANS 15:31

Paul might have buckled under the pressure. He certainly grew weary. He certainly was misunderstood, rejected, and persecuted. He suffered so much. What kept him going? Verse 29 of Colossians 1 says, "To this end I labor, striving according to His working which works in me mightily." He labors, and he strives. That's the way Paul was. Laboring and striving, even when he was laboring and striving for the wrong things, he was absolutely dedicated to the mission. But there is something more extraordinary at work in Paul, something more than sheer willpower or determination.

I tell you willpower will only take you so far. Willpower is overrated. We need something else, something supernatural, something that does not rely upon my limited willpower. What was it? "I strive according to HIS WORKING which works in me mightily." It was not the strength of Paul, but the strength of Christ in Paul, and through this Christ, Paul said, "I can do all things" (Philippians 4:13). All things!

November 22

"The anointing which you have received
from Him abides in you, and you do not need
that anyone teach you."
1 JOHN 2:27

It was God who gave apostles, prophets, evangelists, pastors and teachers to His Ekklesia, to encourage, edify, and establish all of us deeper into Christ. Can the Holy Spirit in John contradict the Holy Spirit in Paul? By no means.

What then? John was the sole survivor of the first twelve apostles, and now he is very old. Naturally he is concerned with the welfare of the Ekklesia after his death. So God comforts John, and then John comforts us, with this truth: even if we do not have access to the apostle, or prophet, or evangelist, or pastor and teacher, we are still instructed inwardly. The Ekklesia that Jesus is building is not dependent upon the great men or women of God. We are grateful to the ministry gifts when we have them, but we are not dependent upon them for our Life. The Life is greater than the ministers through which it may be ministered.

November 23

"God chose what is weak in the
world to shame the strong."
1 CORINTHIANS 1:27 ESV

T he Wisdom of God teaches us differently. This Wisdom tells us that the weak things are chosen to overcome the strong things, and power works concurrently with weakness.

God desires to give you power, but that power only comes through weakness. Any power not obtained through weakness is illegitimate, no matter how spiritual it appears. The only legitimate power is granted to those who have been made weak. Power is birthed in weakness. Many exude a certain "power," but there is not the corresponding weakness. Hence, the power only gives them an occasion for boasting. To remedy this, God has ordained that all who would have His power must first be weakened and made empty – we refer to this as being "broken." The purpose of weakness and suffering is to open the way for His Power. The instrument God uses to weaken us is the Cross. Therefore, the Cross is power through weakness.

November 24

"We were buried with Him through
baptism into death, that just as Christ was raised
from the dead by the glory of the Father, even
so we also should walk in newness of life."
ROMANS 6:4

T he Cross is the means by which God reduces us to Christ, that we may be raised to new Life. What cannot be accomplished in a lifetime of self-effort is easily accomplished in God through the Cross.

We may take many shortcuts along the way and attempt to escape the inevitable, but the day we cease striving and meekly accept the Cross we find everything is done for us.

November 25

"If I go and prepare a place for you,
I will come again and will take you to Myself, that
where I am you may be also."
JOHN 14:3 ESV

J esus said He would prepare a place for us, and would come again, and take us to Himself. "Come to ME," Jesus said. And I believe this "place" He has prepared is IN HIMSELF. He has prepared a Place for us and it is a Place of dwelling and abiding in Himself. "I am the Way, the Truth, and the Life," He says. He has, and He is, this Place prepared for us, and He is the Way into that Place. He is our Destination, He is our Purpose, He is our Promised Land, He is our Sabbath Day, He is our Rest.

So the Ekklesia that Jesus is building, is a spiritual house of living stones. It is the gathering together INTO CHRIST of those who are called out of the earthly, out of the carnal, out of the natural, out of the worldly, out of the fleshly, out of that which is merely human, out of darkness, out of death, and into the spiritual, into the heavenly, into the very Life of God Himself.

November 26

"Of His fullness we have all
received, and grace for grace."
JOHN 1:16

I am frequently asked how do we partake of this fullness? How do we walk in it? What practical application exists for living according to this Truth? We see what God says, but we also see our situation. We see Jesus, but we also see ourselves. God says we are complete in Him, but we say we are incomplete. God says we are blessed with every spiritual blessing in Christ, but we say we still need this or that. What is the problem here? Is it not a glaring discrepancy between what God says and what we say? Whose word is more reliable?

November 27

"God... does not live in temples made by man."
ACTS 17:24 ESV

We are not zealous for the establishment of any earthly nation, but for a heavenly nation of kings and priests (Revelation 5:10). We are not praying for the building of a physical temple, but a spiritual temple, a house of living stones, of which Jesus Christ is the Cornerstone, Builder and Architect. We are not looking for the appearance of an earthly Messiah, but a Heavenly Messiah, Who is building His Ekklesia upon the earth; we are not of the earth. This is not our home, for we are from above. Though in the world, we are not of it. We will not eat its meat or drink its wine, and we will not bow down to its idols. Though we live in the shadow of Babylon, we are not afraid of its fiery furnace or its den of lions, for our God is able to deliver us. The heavens do rule. We affirm it boldly and confidently, regardless of appearances to the contrary. The Kingdom, the Power, and the Glory belongs to God (Matthew 6:13) – not man, not the devil, and not the nations of this world.

November 28

"Blessed be the God and Father
of our Lord Jesus Christ, Who has blessed us
with every spiritual blessing in
heavenly places in Christ."
EPHESIANS 1:3

Most Christians are taught to approach God and seek these things when they are conscious of some lack. Eventually we must learn that we have everything in Christ already. That thing called "patience" that we are so diligently seeking is not a thing at all, it is Christ. "Victory" is no longer a "thing," it is a Man.

And so it is with everything else we need. What a difference it makes to realize that He HAS (past tense) blessed us already – not with three or five or twenty blessings – but with EVERY spiritual blessing. However many there may be, we have them all. Where and how has He done this? Thank God, it was done the moment we received Christ and entered into Him as our All in All. God would have us seek Him first, and not His things. To Him there is no "thing," for they are all summed up into Christ.

November 29

"In due season we shall reap."
GALATIANS 6:9

T he good news is that even if the Ekklesia has been underground, it is still growing and developing. When the season is right it will burst forth and once again those who have eyes to see will indeed discern the blade, the head, and the full grain in the head. In fact the blades have already broken ground in several places and we are even beginning to see some grain taking shape. There have been many obstacles and hindrances to God's Will over the last six thousand years or so of the history of mankind.

So far God has defeated everything that rose up to challenge His Purpose in Christ. Not only has He defeated it, but He has actually used evil to bring about good and further increase His Son. The Scriptures provide us with every expectation and assurance that God will continue to do the same with our generation. He is very much an active part of world affairs, whether they are secular or sacred.

November 30

"He Himself gave some to be
apostles, some prophets, some evangelists,
and some pastors and teachers, for the equipping
of the saints for the work of ministry, for the
edifying of the body of Christ, till we all come
to the unity of the faith and of the knowledge
of the Son of God, to a perfect man,
to the measure of the stature of
the fullness of Christ."
EPHESIANS 4:11-13

Each of these ministry functions fulfill different roles, but their purpose is the same, and that is, to bring ALL of us into that same fullness, that same spiritual maturity, that same experiential knowing, which the elders themselves enjoy. Thus, He gives SOME, till we ALL... SOME, till we ALL... SOME, till we ALL. Do you see this? And He will continue to give SOME till we ALL. Once He has ALL then the work is complete and these ministries will no longer be needed. Until then they ARE needed, and they are critical to God's Purpose.

December 1

"We preach Christ crucified,
to the Jews a stumbling block and to the
Greeks foolishness, but to those who are called,
both Jews and Greeks, Christ is the power of
God and the wisdom of God, because the
foolishness of God is wiser than men."
1 CORINTHIANS 1:23-25

There is tremendous power released in this Cross. Of course, this heavenly power is disguised in earthly weakness, and so it appears to be foolishness to those without understanding. Even Christians often underestimate the comprehensiveness of its work, and mostly think of the Cross in terms of their personal salvation. Certainly that is part of the work of the Cross, but there is far more.

In the Cross we see all the "Kingdom Conundrums" gathered together into one dramatic act. The Cross embodies the ultimate paradox of spiritual life: that wisdom is revealed through foolishness; that giving up is necessary in order to gain; that true strength is found in the midst of weakness; that one must die before they can truly live.

December 2

*"The sacrifices of God are a
broken spirit, a broken and a contrite heart—
these, O God, You will not despise."*
PSALM 51:17

We must never seek the power of Pentecost without first tasting the suffering of the Cross. The Cross is Power disguised in Weakness. There is a saying, "Absolute power corrupts absolutely." We can just as well say that spiritual power obtained apart from the weakness of the Cross will corrupt also. This is why the Lord leads us first to Calvary, then on to Pentecost. We dare not bypass Calvary in our haste to experience Pentecost.

December 3

"For of Him and through Him and to Him are all
things, to Whom be glory forever. Amen."
ROMANS 11:36

The final word is: "Amen – may it be so,
henceforth and forever." We proclaim it,
not to bring it forth (as if it depended upon our
confession), but to acknowledge it as a present
reality which is breaking forth upon all that
stands in opposition to it, and to establish once
and for all that we have chosen – individually
and corporately – to align ourselves with God's
Ultimate Purpose and Will, making us co-
workers together with Him towards the Goal of
CHRIST FILLING ALL THINGS.

He MUST increase, and all else MUST
decrease (John 3:30). We can observe this
decrease taking place in the world around us,
but we should also be able to see that WE, the
Self, is being decreased in order to prepare us
for the Kingdom in which it is no longer "I"
that live as a thing outside of Christ, but it is
Christ Who lives in me, conforming me to His
image, and reproducing His character and
nature within me (Galatians 2:20).

December 4

"Put on the armor of light... put on the
Lord Jesus Christ, and make no provision for the
flesh... put on the whole armor of God."
ROMANS 13:12,14; EPHESIANS 6:11

May I frankly say that anyone trusting in "spiritual armor" as a thing in and of itself is going to fail miserably. Anyone relying upon a faith-formula or a spiritual warfare method is going to see both the formula and the method eventually meet with defeat. Why? Because God has not given us a formula or a method: He has given us His Son.

He does not give us a ritual or ceremony to follow, He says, "Put on the Lord Jesus." Having the Lord Jesus, I have the Whole Armor of God. It is not necessary to ask for each piece of armor, or to confess anything, or to do anything. It is only necessary, having put on the Whole Armor of God, to "stand therefore." It is only necessary, having put on the Lord Jesus, to abide in Him.

December 5

"Father, I desire that they also whom
You gave Me may be with Me..."
JOHN 17:24

You are called to be with Jesus. That is your calling. That is the primary thing, the highest ministry. Going forth to preach or do anything else is of secondary importance. We should be with Jesus; after that, He might send us forth to preach. But before Jesus said, "Go into all the world" He said, "Be with Me."

The call of the Lord is not more important than the Lord of the call. The work of the Lord must not replace the Lord of the work. No amount of ministering FOR the Lord will make up for a lack of ministering TO the Lord. And knowing the Word of God does not necessarily mean that we know the God of the Word.

December 6

"I am the resurrection and
the life. He who believes in Me, though
he may die, he shall live."
JOHN 11:25

The Cross does not represent Death – it represents Life out of Death. Jesus does not refer to Himself as the Crucifixion and the Death, but He calls Himself the Resurrection and the Life. Even so, this Resurrection and Life implies that there has been a very real, thorough death. You cannot resurrect someone who has not died.

God desires that all of us stand together with Christ on resurrection ground where death has no power over us. That is certainly a powerful ground to stand upon, but there is no direct route to get there. The path to resurrection takes us through the Cross, for there can be no Resurrection and Life apart from crucifixion and death.

December 7

"In the world you will have tribulation. But take
heart; I have overcome the world."
JOHN 16:33 ESV

In the world we will experience temptations,
testings, and trials. We will experience
persecution, tribulation, and afflictions of soul
and body. We will experience mistreatment
and misunderstanding. It is not a question of
God allowing or not allowing things to happen.
It is part of living. Some things we do to
ourselves, other things we do to each other.
Our Father knows about every bird which falls
to the ground, but He does not always prevent
it from falling.

What are we to learn from this? That our
response to what happens is more important
than what happens. Here is a mystery: one
man's experience drives him to curse God,
while another man's identical experience drives
him to bless God. Your response to what
happens is more important than what happens.

December 8

"Count it all joy when you
fall into various trials, knowing that the testing
of your faith produces patience."
JAMES 1:2,3

T he Lord does not tempt us with the intent
of making us stumble. That is the way the
adversary works. No, the Lord indeed tests us
and proves us, but His Way is to strengthen us
in the testing, whereas the devil wants to
weaken us in the testing. It has been said that
our circumstances will either leave us better or
they will leave us bitter. Ultimately, the
decision is ours. We should steadfastly resist
the temptation of satan, but we should also
learn to distinguish between the assault of the
enemy and the proving of the Lord.

Jesus already knows what He is going to do.
In His mind it is as good as done. But He waits,
and He proves us. Not because He does not
know us, but because we do not know
ourselves.

December 9

"I will boast all the more gladly
of my weaknesses, so that the power of
Christ may rest upon me."
2 CORINTHIANS 12:9 ESV

If you want to boast, take pride in the things that make you weak, for when you are weak, you are strong – in Him. Be afraid of the praise and acceptance of others, for they are the fertilizer for the self-important and grandiose thoughts that are yours by nature anyway, which spring up in the shallow ground of your carnal mind. Carry about the Death of the Lord so you may have the Life of the Lord. Be ready to suffer with Him, that you may reign with Him.

December 10

"That you, being rooted
and grounded in love, may be able to
comprehend with all the saints what is the width
and length and depth and height—to know the
love of Christ which passes knowledge; that you
may be filled with all the fullness of God."
EPHESIANS 3:17-19

We ought to meditate on this daily and ask the Lord to open our eyes to see the height, depth, width, length, and breadth of this JESUS Whom we say we serve. May God deliver us from our own idea, concept, perception, and illusion of a small Christ and give us revelation into the preeminence of His Son.

When we see Christ as All in All then it will be impossible for us to ever again be reduced to the small, the trivial, the petty things which occupy us and waste so much of our time. Our only hope is seeing a Christ that fills us, a Christ that is greater than us, a Christ that is larger than we can fathom, an indescribable Christ that overshadows, overwhelms, and consumes us through and through!

December 11

"Who being the brightness of
His glory, and the express image of His Person,
and upholding all things by the word of His
power, when He had by Himself purged
our sins, sat down at the right hand
of the Majesty on high."
HEBREWS 1:3

E verything is upheld by His power, and all things are working together according to His Purpose. The Spirit searches all things and reveals them for what they are. Before Him everything is manifest, and there is nothing hidden from Him. There is no darkness that He does not penetrate, no deception that He cannot illuminate, no evil that He will not eradicate.

December 12

"Though I walk through the valley of
the shadow of death, I will fear no evil,
for You are with me."
PSALM 23:4

God ordains that He will walk with us through death. He does not take us around it, or over it, or under it. He does not send us to walk it alone. But He walks with us *through* the valley of the shadow of death.

This is more prophetic than you may realize, for this "valley of the shadow of death" is a reference to the Cross. We fear no evil because the One Who calls us to take up the Cross is right there with us, comforting us with His rod and staff. This death will be the end of something, but it will also be the beginning of something – for death in the Irresistible Kingdom is never the end of the story, it is only the beginning of a new chapter.

December 13

"He who finds his life will lose it, and he who
loses his life for My sake will find it."
MATTHEW 10:39

E ach time you lose a part of your life, you
will find Christ's Life is right there to fill
the void. Every single time. This is a spiritual
truth, and there are no exceptions to the rule.
Think of what it means. The more I give to
Him, the more He gives to me. I trade in my
life in exchange for His Life.

Which would you rather have? Do you want
your life, your failures, your mistakes, your
frustrations, your sins? Or would you rather
give that up in exchange for His Life? You can
have either one you want, but you cannot have
both.

December 14

"[Jesus] went a little farther, and fell on
the ground, and prayed... 'Father, all things are
possible for You. Take this cup away from Me;
nevertheless, not what I will, but what You will."
MARK 14:35,36

True prayer affords us the greatest opportunity for self-denial. When was the last time we offered up prayer, not for our agenda or plan, but for God's Kingdom to come and for God's Will to be done? When was the last time we came before the Lord, not to get our needs met, but to meet His Need? When was the last time we subjugated our own desires and wishes and gave ourselves wholly to praying for God's Purpose to be accomplished? When was the last time we separated ourselves from family, friends, and business and sought the Lord; not to receive a blessing FROM Him, but to be a blessing TO Him?

December 15

"[Jesus] said to them, 'When
you pray, say: 'Our Father in heaven, Hallowed be
Your name. Your kingdom come. Your will be
done on earth as it is in heaven."
LUKE 11:2

This is a revolutionary act. It is praying for the establishment of a Kingdom and a Will in which Christ has the preeminence as All in All. In this Kingdom there is no room for any earthly government, ruler, or king. In this Will there is no room for any human agenda. We know Jesus is Lord, yet we do not see all things submitted to Him (Hebrews 2:8).

So what do we do in the meantime? Overcomers do not just passively wait for Jesus to come back. They pray for His Kingdom to be established and for His Will to be performed. In this way they exercise power over the nations by preparing the way of the Lord. So this prayer is destructive in a natural sense, but constructive in a spiritual sense, for as the nations are decreased, Christ is increased (John 3:30).

December 16

"You meant evil against me;
but God meant it for good."
GENESIS 50:20

And that is the work of the Cross: to be able to see that God is working all things together for good. Even the things that we would not choose! Even the things that we do not like to go through! Even the things that we do not want to experience! Even the evil things that other people do to us! All of these things God can use for our good if we will embrace them and accept them and understand the reason why God permits them to come to us.

Everything we experience: whether it is evil or whether it is good; whether it is something we have not chosen or something that we have chosen; whether it is something we like or something we do not like; all things are working together to increase Christ and decrease us. That is the principle that we see in the life of Joseph.

December 17

"Being in Bethany at the
house of Simon the leper, as He sat at the
table, a woman came having an alabaster flask of
very costly oil of spikenard. Then she broke the
flask and poured it on His head."
MARK 14:3

P erhaps you are in a lonely place because the Lord desires to use you to establish a place in the wilderness for Him. If the Lord has impressed His Need for such a place on your heart, then declare your heart a "Bethany" place and take this up between yourself and the Lord. Give the Lord some ground to build upon. Give Him His place. Do not look for multitudes of people. It is better to have one, two, or three gathered together as the Lord's Bethany than to have hundreds or thousands of people gathered together as something other than Bethany.

Is there anyone in all the world who can truly meet for the purpose of ministering to the Lord and "waste" themselves in worship, giving no thought to their own need, but laying down their lives wholly for the Lord's satisfaction?

December 18

*"The city had no need of the
sun or of the moon to shine in it, for the glory of
God illuminated it. The Lamb is its light."*
REVELATION 21:21

T he spiritual governs the natural, while the natural helps us to interpret the spiritual. When God said, "Let there be light" He established the foundation of the spiritual and the natural world. In the natural world, according to what we can observe, light is increasing the size of our universe infinitely in every direction. But in the spiritual world, the True Light, Jesus Christ, is shining into spiritual darkness with an irresistible, unstoppable brightness.

When God said, "Let there be Light," He was saying, "Let Christ be infinitely increased in all directions at once!" And it was so. He must increase, therefore He will increase, and He is increasing.

December 19

"Beware lest anyone cheat you through
philosophy and empty deceit, according to the
tradition of men, according to the basic principles
of the world, and not according to Christ."
COLOSSIANS 2:8

If by the end of today there is less of me and more of Jesus then I am growing. Otherwise I am not. Jesus must become greater and greater in my life, and I must become lesser and lesser. This is the Path. Along this Path towards apprehending Christ as All in all, there are many pitfalls, snares, hindrances, and detours.

Thus, Paul says we are to be on our guard and let no man cheat us. In this context, the word "cheat" means, "to destroy and strip of one's possessions; to deprive of something valuable by force." Each believer has an incredible fullness and completeness in the Person of Jesus Christ. Christ is THE Gift of God, the ultimate Gift, and this Gift is precious, valuable, and of great worth.

December 20

"The Revelation of Jesus Christ, which
God gave Him to show His servants."
REVELATION 1:1

May God give us the revelation of Christ! Oh God, give us that vision of Him! If we are illuminated to see Him then we cannot remain small any longer. He is God's Answer for smallness.

This Testimony is a boundary-breaking thing, an overshadowing thing, an expansive and increasing thing: "Of the increase of His Government and peace THERE SHALL BE NO END" (Isaiah 9:7). Not only will there be no end of His Kingdom, but there will be no end of HIS INCREASING! Oh God, we cannot fathom that! We cannot comprehend that! It cannot be contained. We cannot take it and fit it into our program. We have to find a way to fit into IT, and not the other way around.

December 21

"[Elisha] said, 'Go, borrow... empty vessels...
then pour [oil] into all those vessels.'"
2 KINGS 4:3,4

There is no lack of supply with the Lord.
There is only a lack of willing vessels. The
oil kept flowing until there were no more
vessels to fill. A willing vessel is both yielded
and empty. A vessel which is unwilling to be
used cannot receive of the Infinite Supply. And
a vessel which is already full cannot receive.
The Life of the Lord is always looking for
expression through a willing vessel that is both
yielded and empty.

December 22

"Most assuredly, I say to you, unless one
is born again, he cannot see the kingdom of
God... unless one is born of water and the Spirit,
he cannot enter the kingdom of God."
JOHN 3:3,5

All of us are familiar with these verses, but we are not so familiar with what they actually mean. To state it simply, being born-again is not the goal, but the first step towards the goal: the goal is the Kingdom of God. We could state it like this: the narrow gate is not the goal, but it is the first thing we must pass through in order to enter the narrow path.

Our goal, and God's goal, is not the gate, or we would not need a path. Though we begin our journey by entering the gate, the goal is at the end of the path, not at the beginning of the path.

December 23

"We are the circumcision, who worship
God in the Spirit, rejoice in Christ Jesus, and have
no confidence in the flesh."
PHILIPPIANS 3:3

We too quickly put our confidence in flesh and blood. It is easier and speedier to have someone tell us, "Yes, you should do this" or "No, you should not do that." The question is not should or should not; the question is, how is the Life instructing you? If we do not know what the Life is telling us, then we should be still and be quiet until we DO know.

But all too often we know well enough what we are to do, and we are looking for a way out of it; or we are trying to get confirmation from this thing or that thing before we will obey. This is why we have a hard time hearing to begin with. How many times does God have to repeat Himself? How many times does He have to confirm something before we will obey? It sounds spiritual and humble to question and wait, but if the Life has already instructed us then any delay on our part is really disobedience.

December 24

"You are worthy, O Lord, to receive glory
and honor and power; for You created all things,
and by Your will they exist and were created."
REVELATION 4:11

All things were created by Him, and everything was created for Him. For Him! Why this earth, the moon, the stars, the galaxies? Why the animals, the birds, the fish, the insects? Why men and women, angels, cherubim, and seraphim? For Him! All for Him!

God's original thought is for Christ to fill every created thing with His Life, Love, and Glory. A design implies a Designer, a plan implies a Planner, and a creation implies a Creator. We are not drifting along aimlessly, and we did not come into being by accident. We were created by Him, and we were created for Him. We were created to love Him, and to be loved by Him.

December 25

"He who did not spare His own Son,
but delivered Him up for us all, how shall He not
with Him also freely give us all things?"
ROMANS 8:32

When God wished to test Abraham, He did not ask him to sacrifice a sheep, a ram, or a cow. He did not ask for Abraham's gold or silver or tents or possessions. He went right to the heart of the matter and asked for Isaac, the son of promise. How gladly Abraham would have given anything and everything but his own beloved son. But in the willingness to give up his son, he was, in essence, laying everything down on the altar. When God owns what the man loves most, He owns everything the man has.

In the same way, the Father, wishing to demonstrate His great love for us, has not given us parts and pieces of things, but has sacrificed His only Son. By giving us His Son, He has, in essence and in fact, freely given us everything. When man possesses what God loves most, he owns everything God has.

December 26

"I do not understand my own actions. For I do not
do what I want, but I do the very thing I hate."
ROMANS 7:15 ESV

W e eventually discover, like Paul, that the
real problem is not what we DO, but
what we ARE. We can confess the same sins
over and over again, or we can take up the
Cross and die to them all. The first approach
deals with sins committed, while the second
approach deals with the sinner.

Which do you think is more effective? Well,
if the one who sins is dead then the issue of
continued sinning becomes irrelevant. Hating
sin is good; hating Self is better, and far more
effective. For the strength of Sin is Self. If you
take the ax to the root of a bad tree, then it will
stop producing bad fruit, and the issue is
settled once and for all. If Self is denied then
Sin becomes superfluous, and the problem of
Evil is solved.

December 27

*"Of His fullness we have all received,
and grace for grace."*
JOHN 1:16

J ust how full is "full"? How many people does "all" include? We have to believe that full means complete, and all includes each one of us. "Of His fullness we have *all* received." No one, no matter how "anointed" they may appear, has more fullness than anyone else. And if we have received it already then there is nothing for us to do to get it.

If I have already entered into a room and sat down in a chair then there is no need for me to try to get into the room anymore. I am there already. We entered into Christ when He entered into us: we do not have to enter into Him over and over again, we are merely abiding in Him.

December 28

"The kingdom of God is as if a man
should scatter seed on the ground, and should
sleep by night and rise by day, and the seed
should sprout and grow, he himself does not
know how. For the earth yields crops by itself:
first the blade, then the head, after that the full
grain in the head. But when the grain ripens,
immediately he puts in the sickle,
because the harvest has come."

MARK 4:26-29

Once the seed is in the ground it just naturally comes forth the way God intended – but not immediately. First the blade, then the head, then the full grain in the head. Like everything else in God's creation, it is progressive.

Likewise, we "do not know how" this Irresistible Kingdom continues to grow and develop, yet it persists in doing so. It really is irresistible. Eventually the harvest will come and we will see the end result. Only then will the magnitude of God's infinite wisdom and the greatness of His Purpose be revealed in all its fullness.

December 29

"The ruler of this world is coming,
and he has nothing in Me."
JOHN 14:30

T he temptations of Christ were not random attempts to trick Him into making a mistake, but were part of a calculated effort to destroy or disqualify Him by any means necessary. From that time on the adversary determined that a direct assault against the Lord Jesus was a pointless waste of time. Why? Because He was so selfless!

You cannot tempt a man who seeks nothing for himself. He wanted nothing and desired nothing but what was given to Him from Above. With Jesus the only option was to destroy Him through the evil intentions of other people. Even in this the Lord Jesus merely passed through crowds who sought to stone Him. He was untouchable and unkillable. Eventually He submitted Himself to betrayal and crucifixion; but even in this He overcame death and rose up in victory. Never before or since has any man so thoroughly routed his enemy. The devil had finally met his match.

December 30

"As we have many members in one body, but
all the members do not have the same function,
so we, being many, are one body in Christ."
ROMANS 12:4,5

There is tremendous authority in the Ekklesia, but it bears repeating: the greater the authority, the greater the responsibility. There is no such thing as authority in the Kingdom of God without responsibility. If God gives you authority to represent Him, there is a reason. Authority is not given to us so we can order people around and make them serve us. Authority is given so we may carry out our own responsibility. There is a task, a function, a mission, an assignment, given to every member of the Ekklesia. Since all the members share in the same authority, all the members share in the same responsibility – though not all share in the same function.

Just as different parts of the body have an equal responsibility to perform their specific function, so the many members of the Body of Christ have equal responsibility to function in the time, place, and manner which is given to them by the authority of the Head.

December 31

"For of Him, and through Him, and to Him,
are all things, to Whom be glory forever. Amen."
ROMANS 11:36

In Romans 11:36 Paul sums up the preeminence of Christ into three expressions: "Of Him... through Him... to Him... are all things."

"Of Him" says that everything which exists – things in heaven, things in earth, everything that was created, everything that has come into being, everything that will come into being – is created by, and because of, Christ. "Through Him" says that everything which lives, moves, breathes, operates, exists, or functions in this universe, whether animate or inanimate, whether biological, chemical, spiritual, natural, or cosmotological – does so through Christ, Who sovereignly upholds all these things, determines their place, and keeps them in order. "To Him" says that everything, no matter how far from God's Thought it may be, no matter how chaotic things may appear, is being directed, summed up, and gathered together into Christ. As the Alpha, all things flow from Him; as the Omega, all things flow to Him.

That is quite a paragraph. A paragraph like that cannot be grasped in one reading. But that paragraph is, in essence, what Paul means, and what we mean, by Christ having the preeminence in all things. We are talking about Jesus as Lord over us individually, over the Ekklesia corporately, and over all creation collectively. We are talking about a preeminent Christ Who is exalted above every principality and power, rule and dominion; things visible, things invisible; things past, things present, things future; things in heaven, things in earth, things under the earth: all things are *of Him*, all things are *through Him*, and all things are *to Him*. That is preeminence.

Inspirational Quotes

Knowing WHAT is a beginning. Knowing WHY is progress. Knowing WHO is maturity.

- CHIP BROGDEN

When you have already lost everything then you have nothing else to lose by telling the truth.

- CHIP BROGDEN

When you get to a place where going back is no longer an option then going back is no longer a temptation.

- CHIP BROGDEN

We have no depth in God because we have no depth of circumstances. Apostolic revelation comes through apostolic persecution.

> - CHIP BROGDEN

There are those who have come to Christ and thanked Him only for what He did, but do not live in the power of who He is.

> - IAN THOMAS

In the Kingdom Economy, Self plus Anything equals Nothing; yet Christ plus Nothing equals Everything.

> - CHIP BROGDEN

It is always good to have mountains to right and left, an enemy behind and the sea in front, for then faith has its opportunity.

> -WATCHMAN NEE

God delights in the impossible because it forces us to rely on Him; otherwise we think we have something to do with it.

> - CHIP BROGDEN

There is a reason why the "Book of Acts" was not named "The Book of Good Intentions."

> - CHIP BROGDEN

It took five hundred years of walking with God, but Noah found grace, and that made it all worthwhile. Let us learn to do nothing apart from this amazing grace. It is better to wait five hundred years for grace than to work for five minutes without it.

> - CHIP BROGDEN

It is not what is done *for* God, but what is done *by* God, that will last.

> - T. AUSTIN-SPARKS

Anyone who serves God will discover sooner or
later that the great hindrance to his work is not
others but himself.

-WATCHMAN NEE

The world is filled with gifted people. We need a
little less giftedness and a lot more brokenness.

-CHIP BROGDEN

The loftiest spiritual service will never take away
from the most mundane earthly responsibility.

- CHIP BROGDEN

The work of the Lord must never become more
important than the Lord of the work.

- CHIP BROGDEN

The Christ we manifest is too small because in
ourselves we have grown too big.

– WATCHMAN NEE

If we can figure out the Lord Jesus then we have
made Him too small. To know Him is to know
how little of Him we know.

- CHIP BROGDEN

The purpose of revelation is not to *substantiate*
your illusions about God, but to *eliminate*
them.

- CHIP BROGDEN

Jesus will not change Who He is in order to
accommodate your thinking; He will change
your thinking to accommodate Who He is.

- CHIP BROGDEN

Sometimes we *are* hearing from God but we just
don't like what He's saying.

- CHIP BROGDEN

Religion seeks to reform a man; the Cross seeks to crucify him. Religion never succeeds yet the Cross never fails.

- CHIP BROGDEN

Prayer doesn't change things, prayer changes *us*; then *we* change things.

- CHIP BROGDEN

It is not always God's will for us to be saved *from* the fire. Often we are called to walk with Him *through* the fire.

- CHIP BROGDEN

There is no lack of supply with the Lord. There is only a lack of willing vessels.

- CHIP BROGDEN

Anyone who puts the Kingdom of God first will soon discover that what God wants is often very different from what people want.

- CHIP BROGDEN

The Testimony of Jesus is not in your mouth, it is in your life. One good deed in His Name is worth more than 1,000 sermons.

- CHIP BROGDEN

People are in a state of spiritual starvation. Don't waste time analyzing the Bread of Life; just give them the Bread.

- CHIP BROGDEN

The significance of the Lord Jesus is not that He can give us bread, but that He *is* the Bread.

- CHIP BROGDEN

Do you have a doctrine? A set of beliefs? Or a Man?
That is the difference between a living
Christianity and a dead religion.

- CHIP BROGDEN

Religion tries to *attain* to something that disciples
of Jesus have already *obtained* in Christ.

- CHIP BROGDEN

Christianity will die, not when everyone rejects the
Gospel, but when everyone accepts a lukewarm
version of it.

- CHIP BROGDEN

Union with Jesus is not the reward for spirituality;
it is the basis of spirituality.

- CHIP BROGDEN

There is no darkness that He does not penetrate, no
deception that He cannot illuminate, no evil
that He will not eradicate.

- CHIP BROGDEN

Spiritual Growth is not more knowledge or increase
of years: it is simply more of Jesus and less of
me.

- CHIP BROGDEN

The Greater is always Greater, and the Lesser is
always Lesser. We only have a problem when
we see everything else as "greater" and see
Christ as "lesser".

- CHIP BROGDEN

If we are one with the Head, we are one with the
Body, even if we are not gathered together. But,
if we are not one with the Head, we are not one
with the Body, even if we are gathered
together.

- CHIP BROGDEN

By establishing His Presence in the midst of just
two or three people, Jesus repudiates our
fascination with large numbers.

-CHIP BROGDEN

A true prophet attends the meeting and suffers in
silence, or stays home and suffers in solitude;
but either way, he suffers.

- CHIP BROGDEN

We've got to be able to say with 100% conviction
that: 1) Jesus is enough; 2) Jesus is all I need;
3) Jesus is all I *want*.

- CHIP BROGDEN

When we know the preciousness and costliness of
the Lord Jesus we will not ask God for anything
else.

- CHIP BROGDEN

To contact the author, obtain additional copies
of this book, or request a complete listing of
books, audio teachings, and other resources
available, please visit our website.

TheSchoolOfChrist.Org